Insights You Need from
Harvard
Business
Review

AGILE

Insights You Need from Harvard Business Review

Business is changing. Will you adapt or be left behind?

Get up to speed and deepen your understanding of the topics that are shaping your company's future with the **Insights You Need from Harvard Business Review** series. Featuring HBR's smartest thinking on fast-moving issues—blockchain, cybersecurity, AI, and more—each book provides the foundational introduction and practical case studies your organization needs to compete today and collects the best research, interviews, and analysis to get it ready for tomorrow.

You can't afford to ignore how these issues will transform the landscape of business and society. The Insights You Need series will help you grasp these critical ideas—and prepare you and your company for the future.

Books in the series include:

Agile

Artificial Intelligence

Blockchain

Climate Change

Customer Data and Privacy

Cybersecurity

Monopolies and Tech Giants

Strategic Analytics

The Year in Tech, 2021

Insights You Need from
Harvard Business Review

AGILE

Harvard Business Review Press
Boston, Massachusetts

HBR Press Quantity Sales Discounts

Harvard Business Review Press titles are available at significant quantity discounts when purchased in bulk for client gifts, sales promotions, and premiums. Special editions, including books with corporate logos, customized covers, and letters from the company or CEO printed in the front matter, as well as excerpts of existing books, can also be created in large quantities for special needs.

For details and discount information for both print and ebook formats, contact booksales@harvardbusiness.org, tel. 800-988-0886, or www.hbr.org/bulksales.

Copyright 2020 Harvard Business School Publishing Corporation

All rights reserved
Printed in the United States of America

10 9 8 7 6 5 4 3 2 1

No part of this publication may be reproduced, stored in or introduced into a retrieval system, or transmitted, in any form, or by any means (electronic, mechanical, photocopying, recording, or otherwise), without the prior permission of the publisher. Requests for permission should be directed to permissions@harvardbusiness.org, or mailed to Permissions, Harvard Business School Publishing, 60 Harvard Way, Boston, Massachusetts 02163.

The web addresses referenced in this book were live and correct at the time of the book's publication but may be subject to change.

Library of Congress Cataloging-in-Publication Data

Title: Agile.
Other titles: Agile (Harvard Business Review Press) | Insights you need from Harvard Business Review.
Description: Boston, Massachusetts : Harvard Business Review Press, [2020] | Series: Insights you need from Harvard Business Review | Includes index.
Identifiers: LCCN 2019046718 (print) | LCCN 2019046719 (ebook) | ISBN 9781633698956 (paperback) | ISBN 9781633698963 (ebook)
Subjects: LCSH: Agile project management. | Business planning. | Strategic planning.
Classification: LCC HD69.P75 A396 2020 (print) | LCC HD69.P75 (ebook) | DDC 658.4—dc23
LC record available at https://lccn.loc.gov/2019046718
LC ebook record available at https://lccn.loc.gov/2019046719

ISBN: 978-1-63369-895-6
eISBN: 978-1-63369-896-3

The paper used in this publication meets the requirements of the American National Standard for Permanence of Paper for Publications and Documents in Libraries and Archives Z39.48-1992.

Contents

Contents

Introduction

AGILE: HOW TO GET IN THE GAME (AND NOT GET IN THE WAY)

by Darrell K. Rigby

Ask general managers what they know about agile, and chances are they'll respond with an uneasy smile and a deflecting quip such as "just enough to be dangerous." They may pepper conversations with terms like "sprints" and "time boxes," use *agile* as an adjective to describe some new initiative, and claim that their businesses are becoming more and more nimble. But because they haven't studied the methodology behind agile practices or seen agile teams in action, they couldn't really tell you what agile is all about or how it's actually working in their organization.

What is agile? It's a mindset and a method for improving innovation through deep customer collaboration and adaptive testing and learning. Here's how it works.

Agile teams are small, cross-functional, fully dedicated work groups focused on creating innovative improvements to customer products and services, the business processes that produce them, and the technologies that enable those processes. Each team has an "owner" who is ultimately responsible for delivering value to customers, and a "coach" who helps the team continuously improve its speed, effectiveness, and happiness. Team members break complex problems into small modules and then start building working versions of potential solutions in short cycles (less than a month) known as sprints. The process is transparent to everyone. Team members hold brief daily "stand-up" meetings to review progress and identify roadblocks. They resolve disagreements through experimentation and feedback rather than endless debates or appeals to authority. They test small working prototypes of part or all of the offering with a few customers for short periods of time. If customers get excited, a prototype may be released immediately, even if some senior executive isn't a fan, or others think it needs more bells and whistles. The team then brainstorms ways to improve future cycles and prepares to attack the next top priority.

When general managers lack this foundational understanding, their everyday ways of working make adoption of agile—and eventual success—nearly impossible. These managers launch countless initiatives with urgent deadlines instead of assigning the highest priority to two or three. They spread themselves and their best people across too many projects rather than concentrating everyone's energy on full-time, focused teams. Many managers become overly involved in the work of project teams. They routinely overturn team decisions and add review layers and controls, trying (usually in vain) to keep mistakes from being repeated but, in the meantime, hampering the speed of innovation. With the best of intentions, they erode the benefits that agile innovation can deliver.

Sound familiar? Too many companies suffer from too much bureaucracy and not enough innovation. Their organizations are unbalanced. Bureaucratic processes originally designed to make successful practices repeatable and scalable have taken over. They have created static business systems—systems that are incapable of adapting to dynamic markets.

The solution to this problem already exists in thousands of companies. Trouble is, it's often hidden inside IT, whose techniques and terminology already intimidate other departments. But the IT folks are onto something: agile has revolutionized technology development over the last 30 years. According to a 2018 survey by the website Stack Overflow, 85% of software developers use agile techniques in their work. Agile increases team productivity and employee satisfaction. It minimizes the waste inherent in redundant meetings, repetitive planning, excessive documentation, quality defects, and low-value product features. By improving visibility and continually adapting to customers' changing priorities, agile boosts customer engagement and satisfaction, brings the most valuable products and features to market faster and more predictably, and reduces risk. When agile engages team members from multiple disciplines as collaborative peers, it broadens organizational experience and builds mutual trust and respect.

Results like these are now driving agile into more functions and industries. Digital natives such as Amazon, Google, Microsoft, Netflix, Riot Games, and Spotify have led the way in scaling agile across a wide range of innovation activities. John Deere, the farm-equipment manufacturer, has used agile methods to develop new machinery. Mission Bell Winery has used them for everything from wine production to warehousing. C. H. Robinson, a global third-party logistics provider, has applied them in human resources. The list goes on. OpenView has used agile to run its venture capital fund; USAA, to transform its customer service; and 3M, to run a major merger integration. Bosch—a global supplier of technology and services with more than 400,000 associates—has adopted agile principles to guide a step-by-step reshaping of the company, including everything from supply-chain management and product development to marketing and strategic planning.

How can your company or team take advantage of agile? This book will help you in two ways. If your organization is adopting or expanding agile practices, it will give you the baseline understanding you need to join in the conversation. It will demystify the concept and build a strong foundation for future learning. At the same time, it will enable you to avoid being an impediment. Sure, agile is sometimes accompanied by off-putting jargon (scrum, kanban), indecipherable acronyms (FROCC, MoSCoW), and zealots who often overstate both its uses and its benefits. At root, though, agile is a simple, practical approach to innovation that every manager can master—and actually enjoy.

To support agile teams, general managers may need to adapt elements of the business's operating model. They have a lot of levers at their disposal: clarifying ambitions; changing leadership styles and cultures; redefining roles and decisions rights; changing planning, budgeting, and reviewing systems; revamping hiring and talent management systems; and increasing the agility of business processes and technologies. Organization structures may need to change as well. Deciding which tools to deploy, in what sequence, and to what degree requires considerable testing, learning, balancing, and customization.

Agile is not a panacea. It is most effective and easiest to implement where the problem to be solved is complex; solutions are initially unknown, and product requirements will most likely change; the work can be modularized; and close collaboration with end users (and rapid feedback from them) is feasible. These conditions exist for many product development functions, marketing projects, strategic-planning activities, supply-chain challenges, and resource allocation decisions. They are less common in routine operations such as plant maintenance, purchasing, sales calls, and accounting.

The greatest impediment to agile success is not the need for better methodologies, more evidence of significant benefits, or proof that agile can work outside IT. It is the mindset and behavior of managers and executives. Those who learn to lead agile's extension into a broader range of business activities will accelerate profitable growth. This book provides a great start.

Further Reading

If you want to dig deeper and further your understanding of agile, I recommend the following titles:

Doing Agile Right: Transformation Without Chaos, by Darrell Rigby, Sarah Elk, and Steve Berez (Boston: Harvard Business Review Press, 2020).

Multipliers, Revised and Updated: How the Best Leaders Make Everyone Smarter, by Liz Wiseman (New York: HarperBusiness, 2017).

The Phoenix Project: A Novel About IT, DevOps, and Helping Your Business Win, 5th anniversary ed., by Gene Kim, Kevin Behr, and George Spafford (Portland, OR: IT Revolution Press, 2018).

The Principles of Product Development Flow: Second Generation Lean Product Development, by Donald G. Reinertsen (Redondo Beach, CA: Celeritas Publishing, 2009).

Scrum: The Art of Doing Twice the Work in Half the Time, by Jeff Sutherland (New York: Crown Publishing Group, 2014).

(continued)

Time, Talent, Energy: Overcome Organizational Drag and Unleash Your Team's Productive Power, by Michael C. Mankins (Boston: Harvard Business Review Press, 2017).

AGILE

AGILE AT SCALE

by Darrell K. Rigby, Jeff Sutherland, and Andy Noble

By now most business leaders are familiar with agile innovation teams. These small, entrepreneurial groups are designed to stay close to customers and adapt quickly to changing conditions. When implemented correctly, they almost always result in higher team productivity and morale, faster time to market, better quality, and lower risk than traditional approaches can achieve.

Naturally, leaders who have experienced or heard about agile teams are asking some compelling questions. What if a company were to launch dozens, hundreds, or even thousands of agile teams throughout the organization? Could whole segments of the business learn to operate in this manner? Would scaling up agile improve corporate performance as much as agile methods improve individual team performance?

In today's tumultuous markets, where established companies are furiously battling assaults from startups and other insurgent competitors, the prospect of a fast-moving, adaptive organization is highly appealing. But as enticing as such a vision is, turning it into a reality can be challenging. Companies often struggle to know which functions should be reorganized into multidisciplinary agile teams and which should not. And it's not unusual to launch hundreds of new agile teams only to see them bottlenecked by slow-moving bureaucracies.

We have studied the scaling up of agile at hundreds of companies, including small firms that run the entire enterprise with agile methods; larger companies that, like Spotify and Netflix, were born agile and have become more so as they've grown; and companies that, like Amazon and USAA (the financial services company for the military community), are making the transition from traditional hierarchies to more-agile enterprises. Along with the many success stories are some disappointments. For example, one prominent industrial company's attempts over the past five years to innovate like a lean startup have not yet generated the financial results sought by activist investors and the board of directors, and several senior executives recently resigned.

Our studies show that companies can scale up agile effectively and that doing so creates substantial benefits. But leaders must be realistic. Not every function needs to be organized into agile teams; indeed, agile methods aren't well suited to some activities. Once you begin launching dozens or hundreds of agile teams, however, you can't just leave the other parts of the business alone. If your newly agile units are constantly frustrated by bureaucratic procedures or a lack of collaboration between operations and innovation teams, sparks will fly from the organizational friction, leading to meltdowns and poor results. Changes are necessary to ensure that the functions that don't operate as agile teams support the ones that do.

Leading Agile by Being Agile

For anyone who isn't familiar with agile, here's a short review. Agile teams are best suited to innovation—that is, the profitable application of creativity to improve products and services, processes, or business models. They are small and multidisciplinary. Confronted with a large, complex problem, they break it into modules, develop solutions to each component through rapid prototyping and tight feedback loops, and integrate the solutions into a coherent whole. They place more value on adapting to change than on sticking to a plan, and they hold themselves accountable for outcomes (such as growth, profitability, and customer loyalty), not outputs (such as lines of code or number of new products).

Conditions are ripe for agile teams in any situation where problems are complex, solutions are at first unclear, project requirements are likely to change, close collaboration with end users is feasible, and creative teams will outperform command-and-control groups. Routine operations such as plant maintenance, purchasing, and accounting are less fertile ground. Agile methods caught on first in IT departments and are now widely used in software development. Over time they have spread into functions such as product development, marketing, and even HR. (See "Embracing Agile," HBR, May 2016, and "HR Goes Agile," HBR, March–April 2018, which appears in chapter 5.)

Agile teams work differently from chain-of-command bureaucracies. They are largely self-governing: Senior leaders tell team members where to innovate but not how. And the teams work closely with customers, both external and internal. Ideally, this puts responsibility for innovation in the hands of those who are closest to customers. It reduces layers of control and approval, thereby speeding up work and increasing the teams' motivation. It also frees up senior leaders to do what only they can do: create and communicate long-term visions, set and sequence strategic priorities, and build the organizational capabilities to achieve those goals.

When leaders haven't themselves understood and adopted agile approaches, they may try to scale up agile the way they have attacked other change initiatives: through top-down plans and directives. The track record is better when they behave like an agile team. That means viewing various parts of the organization as their customers—people and groups whose needs differ, are probably misunderstood, and will evolve as agile takes hold. The executive team sets priorities and sequences opportunities to improve those customers' experiences and increase their success. Leaders plunge in to solve problems and remove constraints rather than delegate that work to subordinates. The agile leadership team, like any other agile team, has an "initiative owner" who is responsible for overall results and a facilitator who coaches team members and helps keep everyone actively engaged.

Bosch, a leading global supplier of technology and services with more than 400,000 associates and operations in 60-plus countries, took this approach. As leaders began to see that traditional top-down management was no longer effective in a fast-moving, globalized world, the company became an early adopter of agile methods. But different business areas required different approaches, and Bosch's first attempt to implement what it called a "dual organization"—one in which hot new businesses were run with agile teams while traditional functions were left out of the action—compromised the goal of a holistic transformation. In 2015 members of the board of management, led by CEO Volkmar Denner, decided to build a more unified approach to agile teams. The board acted as a steering committee and named Felix Hieronymi, a software engineer turned agile expert, to guide the effort.

At first Hieronymi expected to manage the assignment the same way Bosch managed most projects: with a goal, a target completion date, and regular status reports to the board. But that approach felt inconsistent with agile principles, and the company's divisions were just too skeptical of yet another centrally organized program. So the team shifted gears. "The steering committee turned into a working committee," Hieronymi told us. "The discussions got far more interactive." The team compiled and rank-ordered a backlog of corporate priorities that was regularly updated, and it focused on steadily removing companywide barriers to greater agility. Members fanned out to engage division leaders in dialogue. "Strategy evolved from an annual project to a continuous process," Hieronymi says. "The members of the management board divided themselves into small agile teams and tested various approaches—some with a 'product owner' and an 'agile master'—to tackle tough problems or work on fundamental topics. One group, for instance, drafted the 10 new leadership principles released in 2016. They personally experienced the satisfaction of increasing speed and effectiveness. You can't gain this experience by reading a book." Today Bosch operates with a mix of agile teams and traditionally structured units. But it reports that nearly all areas have adopted agile values, are collaborating more effectively, and are adapting more quickly to increasingly dynamic marketplaces.

Getting Agile Rolling

At Bosch and other advanced agile enterprises, the visions are ambitious. In keeping with agile principles, however, the leadership team doesn't plan every detail in advance. Leaders recognize that they do not yet know how many agile teams they will require, how quickly they should add them, and how they can address bureaucratic constraints without throwing the organization into chaos. So they typically launch an initial wave of agile teams, gather data on the value those teams create and the constraints they face, and then decide whether, when, and how to take the next step. This lets them weigh the value of increasing agility (in terms of financial results, customer outcomes, and employee performance) against its costs (in terms of both financial investments and organizational challenges). If the benefits outweigh the costs, leaders continue to scale up agile—deploying another wave of teams, unblocking constraints in less agile parts of the organization, and repeating the cycle. If not, they can pause, monitor the market environment, and explore ways to increase the value of the agile teams already in place (for instance, by improving the prioritization of work or upgrading prototyping capabilities) and decrease the costs of change (by publicizing agile successes or hiring experienced agile enthusiasts).

To get started on this test-and-learn cycle, leadership teams typically employ two essential tools: a taxonomy of potential teams and a sequencing plan reflecting the company's key priorities. Let's first look at how each can be employed and then explore what more is needed to tackle large-scale, long-term agile initiatives.

Create a taxonomy of teams

Just as agile teams compile a backlog of work to be accomplished in the future, companies that successfully scale up agile usually begin by creating a full taxonomy of opportunities. Following agile's modular approach, they may break the taxonomy into three components—customer experience teams, business process teams, and technology systems teams—and then integrate them. The first component identifies all the experiences that could significantly affect external and internal customer decisions, behaviors, and satisfaction. These can usually be divided into a dozen or so major experiences (for example, one of a retail customer's major experiences is to buy and pay for a product), which in turn can be divided into dozens of more-specific experiences (the customer may need to choose a payment method, use a coupon, redeem loyalty points, complete the checkout process, and get a receipt). The second component examines the relationships among these experiences and key business processes (improved checkout to reduce time in lines, for instance), aiming to reduce overlapping responsibilities and increase collaboration between process teams and customer experience teams. The third focuses on developing technology systems (such as better mobile-checkout apps) to improve the processes that will support customer experience teams.

The taxonomy of a $10 billion business might identify anywhere from 350 to 1,000 or more potential teams. Those numbers sound daunting, and senior executives are often loath even to consider so much change. ("How about if we try two or three of these things and see how it goes?") But the value of a taxonomy is that it encourages exploration of a transformational vision while breaking the journey into small steps that can be paused, turned, or halted at any time. It also helps leaders spot constraints. Once you've identified the teams you could launch and the sorts of people you would need to staff them, for instance, you need to ask: Do we have those people? If so, where are they? A taxonomy reveals your talent gaps and the kinds of people you must hire or retrain to fill them. Leaders can also see how each potential team fits into the goal of delivering better customer experiences.

USAA has more than 500 agile teams up and running and plans to add 100 more in 2018. The taxonomy is fully visible to everyone across the enterprise. "If you don't have a really good taxonomy, you get redundancy and duplication," COO Carl Liebert told us. "I want to walk into an auditorium and ask, 'Who owns the member's change-of-address experience?' And I want a clear and confident response from a team that owns that experience, whether a member is calling us, logging in to our website on a laptop, or using our mobile app. No finger-pointing. No answers that begin with 'It's complicated.'"

USAA's taxonomy ties the activities of agile teams to the people responsible for business units and product lines. The goal is to ensure that managers responsible for specific parts of the P&L understand how cross-functional teams will influence their results. The company has senior leaders who act as general managers in each line of business and are fully accountable for business results. But those leaders rely on customer-focused, cross-organizational teams to get much of the work done. The company also depends on technology and digital resources assigned to the experience owners; the goal here is to ensure that business leaders have the end-to-end resources to deliver the outcomes they have committed to. The intent of the taxonomy is to clarify how to engage the right people in the right work without creating confusion. This kind of link is especially important when hierarchical organizational structures do not align with customer behaviors. For example, many companies have separate structures and P&Ls for online and offline operations—but customers want seamlessly integrated omnichannel experiences. A clear taxonomy that launches the right cross-organizational teams makes such alignment possible.

Sequence the transition

Taxonomy in hand, the leadership team sets priorities and sequences initiatives. Leaders must consider multiple criteria, including strategic importance, budget limitations, availability of people, return on investment, cost of delays, risk levels, and interdependencies among teams. The most important—and the most frequently overlooked—are the pain points felt by customers and employees on the one hand and the organization's capabilities and constraints on the other. These determine the right balance between how fast the rollout should proceed and how many teams the organization can handle simultaneously.

A few companies, facing urgent strategic threats and in need of radical change, have pursued big-bang, everything-at-once deployments in some units. For example, in 2015 ING Netherlands anticipated rising customer demand for digital solutions and increasing incursions by new digital competitors ("fintechs"). The management team decided to move aggressively. It dissolved the organizational structures of its most innovative functions, including IT development, product management, channel management, and marketing—essentially abolishing everyone's job. Then it created small agile "squads" and required nearly 3,500 employees to reapply for 2,500 re-designed positions on those squads. About 40% of the people filling the positions had to learn new jobs, and all had to profoundly change their mindset.

But big-bang transitions are hard. They require total leadership commitment, a receptive culture, enough talented and experienced agile practitioners to staff hundreds of teams without depleting other capabilities, and highly prescriptive instruction manuals to align everyone's approach. They also require a high tolerance of risk, along with contingency plans to deal with unexpected breakdowns. ING continues to iron out wrinkles as it expands agile throughout the organization.

Companies short on those assets are better off rolling out agile in sequenced steps, with each unit matching the implementation of opportunities to its capabilities. At the beginning of its agile initiative, the advanced technology group at 3M Health Information Systems launched 8 to 10 teams every month or two; now, two years in, more than 90 teams are up and running. 3M's Corporate Research Systems Lab got started later but launched 20 teams in three months.

Whatever the pace or endpoint, results should begin showing up quickly. Financial results may take a while—Jeff Bezos believes that most initiatives take five to seven years to pay dividends for Amazon—but positive changes in customer behavior and team problem solving provide early signs that initiatives are on the right track. "Agile adoption has already enabled accelerated product deliveries and the release of a beta application six months earlier than originally planned," says Tammy Sparrow, a senior program manager at 3M Health Information Systems.

Division leaders can determine the sequencing just as any agile team would. Start with the initiatives that offer potentially the greatest value and the most learning. SAP, the enterprise software company, was an early scaler of agile, launching the process a decade ago. Its leaders expanded agile first in its software development units—a highly customer-centric segment where they could test and refine the approach. They established a small consulting group to train, coach, and embed the new way of working, and they created a results tracker so that everyone could see the teams' gains. "Showing concrete examples of impressive productivity gains from agile created more and more pull from the organization," says Sebastian Wagner, who was then a consulting manager in that group. Over the next two years the company rolled out agile to more than 80% of its development organizations, creating more than 2,000 teams. People in sales and marketing saw the need to adapt in order to keep up, so those areas went next. Once the front end of the business was moving at speed, it was time for the back end to make the leap, so SAP shifted its group working on internal IT systems to agile.

Too many companies make the mistake of going for easy wins. They put teams into offsite incubators. They intervene to create easy workarounds to systemic obstacles. Such coddling increases the odds of a team's success, but it doesn't produce the learning environment or organizational changes necessary to scale dozens or hundreds of teams. A company's early agile teams carry the burden of destiny. Testing them, just like testing any prototype, should reflect diverse, realistic conditions. Like SAP, the most successful companies focus on vital customer experiences that cause the greatest frustrations among functional silos.

Still, no agile team should launch unless and until it is ready to begin. *Ready* doesn't mean planned in detail and guaranteed to succeed. It means that the team is:

- Focused on a major business opportunity with a lot at stake

- Responsible for specific outcomes

- Trusted to work autonomously—guided by clear decision rights, properly resourced, and staffed with a small group of multidisciplinary experts who are passionate about the opportunity

- Committed to applying agile values, principles, and practices

- Empowered to collaborate closely with customers

- Able to create rapid prototypes and fast feedback loops

- Supported by senior executives who will address impediments and drive adoption of the team's work

Following this checklist will help you plot your sequence for the greatest impact on both customers and the organization.

Master large-scale agile initiatives

Many executives have trouble imagining that small agile teams can attack large-scale, long-term projects. But in principle there is no limit to the number of agile teams you can create or how large the initiative can be. You can establish "teams of teams" that work on related initiatives—an approach that is highly scalable. Saab's aeronautics business, for instance, has more than 100 agile teams operating across software, hardware, and fuselage for its Gripen fighter jet—a $43 million item that is certainly one of the most complex products in the world. It coordinates through daily team-of-teams stand-ups. At 7:30 a.m. each frontline agile team holds a 15-minute meeting to flag impediments, some of which cannot be resolved within that team. At 7:45 the impediments requiring coordination are escalated to a team of teams, where leaders work to either settle or further escalate issues. This approach continues, and by 8:45 the executive action team has a list of the critical issues it must resolve to keep progress on track. Aeronautics also coordinates its teams through a common rhythm of three-week sprints, a project master plan that is treated as a living document, and the colocation of traditionally disparate parts of the organization—for instance, putting test pilots and simulators with development teams. The results are dramatic: IHS Jane's has deemed the Gripen the world's most cost-effective military aircraft.

Building Agility Across the Business

Expanding the number of agile teams is an important step toward increasing the agility of a business. But equally important is how those teams interact with the rest of the organization. Even the most advanced agile enterprises—Amazon, Spotify, Google, Netflix, Bosch, Saab, SAP, Salesforce, Riot Games, Tesla, and SpaceX, to name a few—operate with a mix of agile teams and traditional structures. To ensure that bureaucratic functions don't hamper the work of agile teams or fail to adopt and commercialize the innovations developed by those teams, such companies constantly push for greater change in at least four areas.

Values and principles

A traditional hierarchical company can usually accommodate a small number of agile teams sprinkled around the organization. Conflicts between the teams and conventional procedures can be resolved through personal interventions and workarounds. When a company launches several hundred agile teams, however, that kind of ad hoc accommodation is no longer possible. Agile teams will be pressing ahead on every front. Traditionally structured parts of the organization will fiercely defend the status quo. As with any change, skeptics can and will produce all kinds of antibodies that attack agile, ranging from refusals to operate on an agile timetable ("Sorry, we can't get to that software module you need for six months") to the withholding of funds from big opportunities that require unfamiliar solutions.

So a leadership team hoping to scale up agile needs to instill agile values and principles throughout the enterprise, including the parts that do not organize into agile teams. This is why Bosch's leaders developed new leadership principles and fanned out throughout the company: They wanted to ensure that everyone understood that things would be different and that agile would be at the center of the company's culture.

Operating architectures

Implementing agile at scale requires modularizing and then seamlessly integrating workstreams. For example, Amazon can deploy software thousands of times a day because its IT architecture was designed to help developers make fast, frequent releases without jeopardizing the firm's complex systems. But many large companies, no matter how fast they can code programs, can deploy software only a few times a day or a week; that's how their architecture works.

Building on the modular approach to product development pioneered by Toyota, Tesla meticulously designs interfaces among the components of its cars to allow each module to innovate independently. Thus the bumper team can change anything as long as it maintains stable interfaces with the parts it affects. Tesla is also abandoning traditional annual release cycles in favor of real-time responses to customer feedback. CEO Elon Musk says that the company makes about 20 engineering changes a week to improve the production and performance of the Model S. Examples include new battery packs, updated safety and autopilot hardware, and software that automatically adjusts the steering wheel and seat for easier entry and exit.

In the most advanced agile enterprises, innovative product and process architectures are attacking some of the thorniest organizational constraints to further scaling. Riot Games, the developer of the wildly successful multiplayer online battle arena League of Legends, is redesigning the interfaces between agile teams and support-and-control functions that operate conventionally, such as facilities, finance, and HR. Brandon Hsiung, the product lead for this ongoing initiative, says it involves at least two key steps. One is shifting the functions' definition of their customers. "Their customers are not their functional bosses, or the CEO, or even the board of directors," he explains. "Their customers are the development teams they serve, who ultimately serve our players." The company instituted Net Promoter surveys to collect feedback on whether those customers would recommend the functions to others and made it plain that dissatisfied customers could sometimes hire outside providers. "It's the last thing we want to happen, but we want to make sure our functions develop world-class capabilities that could compete in a free market," Hsiung says.

Riot Games also revamped how its corporate functions interact with its agile teams. Some members of corporate functions may be embedded in agile teams, or a portion of a function's capacity may be dedicated to requests from agile teams. Alternatively, functions might have little formal engagement with the teams after collaborating with them to establish certain boundaries. Says Hsiung: "Silos such as real estate and learning and development might publish philosophies, guidelines, and rules and then say, 'Here are our guidelines. As long as you operate within them, you can go crazy; do whatever you believe is best for our players.'"

In companies that have scaled up agile, the organization charts of support functions and routine operations generally look much as they did before, though often with fewer management layers and broader spans of control as supervisors learn to trust and empower people. The bigger changes are in the ways functional departments work. Functional priorities are necessarily more fully aligned with corporate strategies. If one of the company's key priorities is improving customers' mobile experience, that can't be number 15 on finance's funding list or HR's hiring list. And departments such as legal may need buffer capacity to deal with urgent requests from high-priority agile teams.

Over time even routine operations with hierarchical structures are likely to develop more-agile mindsets. Of course, finance departments will always manage budgets, but they don't need to keep questioning the decisions of the owners of agile initiatives. "Our CFO constantly shifts accountability to empowered agile teams," says Ahmed Sidky, the head of development management at Riot Games. "He'll say, 'I am not here to run the finances of the company. You are, as team leaders. I'm here in an advisory capacity.' In the day-to-day organization, finance partners are embedded in every team. They don't control what the teams do or don't do. They are more like finance coaches who ask hard questions and provide deep expertise. But ultimately it's the team leader who makes decisions, according to what is best for Riot players."

Some companies, and some individuals, may find these trade-offs hard to accept and challenging to implement. Reducing control is always scary—until you do so and find that people are happier and success rates triple. In a Bain survey of nearly 1,300 global executives, more respondents agreed with this statement about management than with any other: "Today's business leaders must trust and empower people, not command and control them." (Only 5% disagreed.)

Talent acquisition and motivation

Companies that are scaling up agile need systems for acquiring star players and motivating them to make teams better. (Treat your stars unfairly, and they will bolt to a sexy startup.) They also need to unleash the wasted potential of more-typical team members and build commitment, trust, and joint accountability for outcomes. There's no practical way to do this without changing HR procedures. A company can no longer hire purely for expertise, for instance; it now needs expertise combined with enthusiasm for work on a collaborative team. It can't evaluate people according to whether they hit individual objectives; it now needs to look at their performance on agile teams and at team members' evaluations of one another. Performance assessments typically shift from an annual basis to a system that provides relevant feedback and coaching every few weeks or months. Training and coaching programs encourage the development of cross-functional skills customized to the needs of individual employees. Job titles matter less and change less frequently with self-governing teams and fewer hierarchical levels. Career paths show how product owners—the individuals who set the vision and own the results of an agile team—can continue their personal development, expand their influence, and increase their compensation.

Companies may also need to revamp their compensation systems to reward group rather than individual accomplishments. They need recognition programs that celebrate contributions immediately. Public recognition is better than confidential cash bonuses at bolstering agile values—it inspires recipients to improve even further, and it motivates others to emulate the recipients' behaviors. Leaders can also reward "A" players by engaging them in the most vital opportunities, providing them with the most advanced tools and the greatest possible freedom, and connecting them with the most talented mentors in their field.

Annual planning and budgeting cycles

In bureaucratic companies, annual strategy sessions and budget negotiations are powerful tools for aligning the organization and securing commitments to stretch goals. Agile practitioners begin with different assumptions. They see that customer needs change frequently and that breakthrough insights can occur at any time. In their view, annual cycles constrain innovation and adaptation: Unproductive projects burn resources until their budgets run out, while critical innovations wait in line for the next budget cycle to compete for funding.

In companies with many agile teams, funding procedures are different. Funders recognize that for two-thirds of successful innovations, the original concept will change significantly during the development process. They expect that teams will drop some features and launch others without waiting for the next annual cycle. As a result, funding procedures evolve to resemble those of a venture capitalist. VCs typically view funding decisions as opportunities to purchase options for further discovery. The objective is not to instantly create a large-scale business but, rather, to find a critical component of the ultimate solution. This leads to a lot of apparent failures but accelerates and reduces the cost of learning. Such an approach works well in an agile enterprise, vastly improving the speed and efficiency of innovation.

. . .

Companies that successfully scale up agile see major changes in their business. Scaling up shifts the mix of work so that the business is doing more innovation relative to routine operations. The business is better able to read changing conditions and priorities, develop adaptive solutions, and avoid the constant crises that so frequently hit traditional hierarchies. Disruptive innovations will come to feel less disruptive and more like adaptive business as usual. The scaling up also brings agile values and principles to business operations and support functions, even if many routine activities remain. It leads to greater efficiency and productivity in some of the business's big cost centers. It improves operating architectures and organizational models to enhance coordination between agile teams and routine operations. Changes come on line faster and are more responsive to customer needs. Finally, the business delivers measurable improvements in outcomes—not only better financial results but also greater customer loyalty and employee engagement.

Agile's test-and-learn approach is often described as incremental and iterative, but no one should mistake incremental development processes for incremental thinking. SpaceX, for example, aims to use agile innovation to begin transporting people to Mars by 2024, with the goal of establishing a self-sustaining colony on the planet. How will that happen? Well, people at the company don't really know . . . yet. But they have a vision that it's possible, and they have some steps in mind. They intend to dramatically improve reliability and reduce expenses, partly by reusing rockets much like airplanes. They intend to improve propulsion systems to launch rockets that can carry at least 100 people. They plan to figure out how to refuel in space. Some of the steps include pushing current technologies as far as possible and then waiting for new partners and new technologies to emerge.

That's agile in practice: big ambitions and step-by-step progress. It shows the way to proceed even when, as is so often the case, the future is murky.

TAKEAWAYS

Once you've seen what agile can do, you'll want to incorporate it into more parts of your organization. How do you know which functions should be reorganized into multidisciplinary agile teams and which should not? And how can you launch several new teams without creating bottlenecks or being hampered by bureaucracy? Take these steps to ensure a successful scaling up at your organization:

✓ Don't just create agile teams; integrate agile methodologies and values into your work, such as viewing different parts of your organization as customers.

✓ Create a taxonomy of opportunities to set priorities.

✓ Break workstreams into modules for seamless integration.

✓ Take a VC-like approach to funding when it's time to begin your annual budgeting process.

Reprinted from Harvard Business Review, *May–June 2018 (product #R1803F).*

WHY AGILE GOES AWRY

by Lindsay McGregor and Neel Doshi

I n the spirit of becoming more adaptive, organizations have rushed to implement agile software development. But many have done so in a way that actually makes them less agile. These companies have become agile in name only, as the process they've put in place often ends up hurting engineering motivation and productivity.

Agile Software Development

Frameworks for adaptive software development like agile have been around for a long time and have manifested in many forms. But at the heart of most of these models are two things: forming hypotheses (for example, what is a feature supposed to accomplish?) and collaborating across domains of expertise on experiments, all in the spirit of driving learning and not careening down a path that proves to be incorrect.

When Agile was born in 2001, it articulated a set of four critical principles to elevate the craft of software development and improve engineering and product manager motivation.

1. Individuals and interactions over processes and tools

2. Working software over comprehensive documentation

3. Customer collaboration over contract negotiation

4. Responding to change over following a plan

In our research on human motivation, we have analyzed the practices of engineers across over 500 different organizations using a combination of survey-based and experimental approaches. We've found that what happens in practice wildly departs from these stated principles.

For example, in common practice, *processes and tools* have become the driver of work, not *individuals and interactions*. In one large *Fortune* 100 company, the head of digital products said to us, "We're not allowed to question the agile process." In another *Fortune* 500 organization, product managers and engineers communicated exclusively through their tools, which were used primarily for the former to issue commands to the latter.

Similarly, documentation often trumps working software. In one large tech company, its product team focused significant up-front time writing small requirements (called "user stories"). These requirements were put into a ticket queue as tasks for the next available engineer to start working on. The bar for documentation to keep the queue moving became high. Ultimately, this process became one of many small "waterfalls," where work is passed from a product department to designers to engineering. This process is exactly what agile was meant to eliminate. It is no wonder that the CTO of this company said, "My engineers feel like short-order cooks in the back of a diner."

When it comes to "responding to change over following a plan," this often gets misinterpreted to mean "don't have a plan." For example, in one fast-growing tech company, the agile teams did not try to understand the broader strategy of the organization. As a result, their attempts to iterate often focused on low-value or strategically unimportant features. Without a plan, teams won't know how to prioritize actions, and how to invest in those actions responsibly. This principle has gone so far as to let engineers believe that it is not appropriate to have time boxes or common milestones.

It would be one thing if these misapplications actually improved engineering motivation and performance, but we have found that in practice, the opposite happens. Agile, when practiced as we've described, reduces the total motivation of engineers. Because they're not allowed to experiment, manage their own work, and connect with customers, they feel little sense of play, potential, and purpose; instead they feel emotional and economic pressure to succeed, or inertia. They stop adapting, learning, and putting their best efforts into their work.

For example, one venture capital partner shared with us a story of how a video game development company continued to build a product for a year, despite every engineer feeling like the game was not worth playing. The company realized it wasted a lot of time and money.

Agile processes go awry, because as companies strive for high performance, they become either too tactical (focusing too much on process and micromanagement) or too adaptive (avoiding long-term goals, timelines, or cross-functional collaboration).

The key is balancing both tactical and adaptive performance. Whether you're an engineer or product manager, here are a few changes to consider for finding this balance, so you can improve your engineering (or any) team's motivation and performance.

Software Development Should Be a No-Handoff, Collaborative Process

Rather than a process where one person writes requirements (even small ones) while another executes them, all without a guiding strategic North Star, a team striving for true agility should have a *no-handoff* process versus a process where one person writes requirements while the other executes them. In a no-handoff process, the product manager and the engineers (and any other stakeholders) are collaborative partners from beginning to end in designing a feature.

First the team, including executives, should articulate the team's strategic challenges. Challenges take the form of a question, always focused on improving some kind of customer outcome or impact. Think of them as a team's detailed mission in question form to trigger expansive thinking. The challenges themselves are developed and iterated by the whole team, including its executive sponsors (and customers). Every single person on the team (or any team for that matter) is asked to contribute ideas to each challenge whenever they want.

For example, in one bank, a challenge was, "How can we help customers be better prepared for possible financial shocks?" Another was, "How can we make it more fun and less of a chore for customers to maintain healthy financial habits?" These challenges produced dozens of ideas from many different people.

Then, instead of someone writing requirements while another person executes, these teams develop and mature an idea collaboratively, from rough draft to testable hypothesis.

The Team's Unit of Delivery Should Be Minimally Viable Experiments

Teams often find they waste time by adapting too much. To avoid this, not only should ideas be formed for a strategic challenge, they should also be executed with fast experiments aimed at learning just enough to know what works for customers. Teams should be maximizing their "speed to truth."

In order to reduce wasted effort and increase the team's decision rights, experiments should be short in nature. If possible, an experiment should be no longer than a week.

Sometimes this requires the team to minimize a feature to what is absolutely needed to test its weakest assumption. Sometimes it means that the team doesn't code but instead completes an offline experiment through research.

The Team's Approach Should Be Customer-Centric

The process of building software (even internal-use software) should be squarely customer-centric.

At the simplest, these principles should cover the following:

- Challenges are always framed around customer impact.

- Problem-solving meetings always start with a customer update, and representatives from the front line are included frequently in these discussions.

- Every experiment is built around a customer-centric hypothesis. That way, the team can hold itself accountable to the outcome predicted by the experiment.

However, even more important is that engineers see with their own eyes how customers use their products. This requires the frontline reps and the engineers working together to see if the product is creating customer impact.

Use Time Boxes to Focus Experimentation and Avoid Waste

Interestingly, adaptive software development encourages time boxes as a way to ensure an experiment is given the investment that is justified and to signal the acceptable quality level of a given feature. On the other hand, typical agile practitioners avoid time boxes or deadlines, for fear that the deadline will be used to create emotional pressure. One of the worst feelings for a software developer is spending a few months working on something that ends up being not useful. This fills you with emotional pressure ("I let everyone down") and a sense of inertia ("Why am I even doing this?").

To avoid this outcome, be clear about how far an engineer should go before checking to see if the direction is still correct. The greater the uncertainty on a team's hypothesis, and the greater the risk, the shorter that runway should be. With that in mind, the time box isn't a deadline. It is a constraint that should guide the level of depth and quality for an experiment before a real test. In this way, time boxes can increase total motivation.

The Team Should Be Organized to Emphasize Collaboration

To make sure you end up with a no-handoff process, the various stakeholders involved should function as a single cross-functional team, also known as a pod. The goal of the pod is to drive collaboration. Each pod should contain the full set of experts needed to deliver a great product. This may include senior executives. In one organization, for example, product pods include a product manager, a front-end engineer, a back-end engineer, a designer, a quality engineer, and part-time representation from customer service, and a senior executive from a control function.

In many organizations, there are telltale signs of "faux" pods—teams that call themselves pods but don't actually operate that way. Signs of faux pods include:

- Experts are in separate, aligned teams, not the same team. For example, a product team has dedicated engineering "sprint teams." These are not pods.

- The team uses tools that prevent real collaboration. For example, when we asked one engineering team's members why they chose the agile software tools they were using, they said, "These tools will *prevent* executives from engaging in our work." All this does is perpetuate a cycle of mistrust.

- Engineering and product functions actually have different goals from the top. Executives in both functions use their hierarchical power to get their people to prioritize the function's goals above all others, including their pod's goals. These conflicts ultimately result in clashes in the working teams that prevent true teamwork.

- Rigidly hierarchical talent processes, like performance ratings, hierarchical titles, pressure to get promoted, and up-or-out systems, destroy the teamwork required to make pods function well. These systems will either make team members more beholden to their boss than their team's customer or put team members in competition with each other. Either way, they will not function as a team.

The stronger an organization's silos, the more people will solve for the needs of their silo versus the needs of their team. This makes collaboration and consensus very difficult to achieve without constant escalation.

The Team Should Constantly Question Its Process

A famous maxim of engineering design is known as Conway's law. It states that *any organization that designs a system will produce a design whose structure is a copy of the organization's communication (that is, process) structure.* Basically, if you're a monolithic organization, you'll produce monolithic designs. If you're organized by user segments, your product will optimize for that structure.

If you want to defeat Conway's law, the better practice is to constantly adjust your structure and processes to suit the problem at hand. This requires teams that have simple, lightweight processes and structures that they constantly question and tweak.

Thus, rather than creating agile as a religion that cannot be questioned, engineering teams should be in the habit of constantly diagnosing and iterating their own team's operating model. In the best examples we've seen, on a monthly basis, teams diagnose their operating model and decide if it needs changing to produce a better product.

. . .

The ability to attract, inspire, and retain digital product talent is becoming mission critical for organizations. Most have fallen prey to a simple message—implement agile as a series of ceremonies and everything gets better. Unfortunately, this is often not the case when the human side of the equation is lost. By getting back to the basics of motivation and adaptive performance, you can build an organization that is truly agile.

TAKEAWAYS

In the rush to become more adaptive, some companies have implemented agile in a way that actually makes them *less* agile, like misinterpreting "responding to change over following a plan" to mean "we don't need a plan." To be agile in more than name only:

✓ Develop a no-handoff process where the product manager, engineers, and other stakeholders collaborate from beginning to end.

✓ Create teams that contain the full set of experts needed to deliver on your goal—from senior executives to part-time customer service reps.

✓ Focus on short experiments (no longer than a week) to reduce wasted effort and increase the team's decision rights.

✓ Keep customers at the center of everything—from observing them using products to starting every meeting with customer updates.

✓ Use time boxes to guide the level of depth and quality for experiments.

Reprinted from hbr.org, originally published October 1, 2018 (product #H04KA0).

3

HOW TO MAKE SURE AGILE TEAMS CAN WORK TOGETHER

by Alia Crocker, Rob Cross, and Heidi K. Gardner

Increasing volatility, uncertainty, growing complexity, and ambiguous information (VUCA) have created a business environment in which agile collaboration is more critical than ever. Organizations need to be continually on the lookout for new market developments and competitive threats, identifying essential experts and nimbly forming and disbanding teams to help tackle those issues quickly. However, these cross-functional groups often bump up against misaligned incentives, hierarchical decision making, and cultural rigidities, causing progress to stall or action to not be taken at all.

Consider the case of an organization in our consortium, the Connected Commons, that uncovered a groundbreaking audiovisual technology that would differentiate the organization in existing channels but also had the potential to open up entirely new markets. The CEO heralded it as a pivot point in growth and formed a cross-functional initiative of 100-plus top employees to bring it to new commercial channels. Yet, unfortunately, progress did not match expectations. Employees assigned to the effort struggled to make time for the work. They often did not understand the expertise or values of different functions and advocated too aggressively for their own solutions. The group was surprised several times by the demands of external stakeholders. Despite this project's visibility, critical mandate, and groundbreaking technology, the organization was ultimately hindered when it came to agile collaboration. This story is not unique.

A significant part of the problem is that work occurs through collaboration in networks of relationships that often do not mirror formal reporting structures or standard work processes. Intuitively, we know that the collaborative intensity of work has skyrocketed, and that collaborations are central to agility. Yet most organizations don't manage internal collaboration productively and assume that technology or formal org charts can yield agility. These efforts often fail because they lack informal networks—for example, employees who share an interest in a technological innovation like artificial intelligence or a passion for environmental sustainability, and who can bridge the organization's entrepreneurial and operational systems by bringing cutting-edge ideas to people who have the resources to begin experimenting and implementing them.

Our research focuses on agility not as a broad ideal but, rather, on where agility matters most—at the point of execution, where teams are working on new products, strategic initiatives, or with top clients. All of these points of execution are essential for organizations, yet all encounter inefficiencies unless they're managed as a network. We assessed these strategically important groups in a wide range of global organizations via network surveys, which were completed by more than 30,000 employees. We also conducted hundreds of interviews with both workers and leaders in these companies. We found that agility at the point of execution is typically created through group-level networks such as account or new product development teams formed with employees drawn from the whole organization, lateral networks across core work processes, temporary teams and task forces formed to drive a critical organizational change or respond to a strategic threat, and communities of practice that enabled organizations to enjoy true benefits of scale. These and other lateral networks provide agility when they are nurtured along four dimensions—managing the center of the network, engaging the fringe, bridging select silos, and leveraging boundary spanners. Leaders who nurture their internal networks in this way produce better outcomes—financial, strategic, and talent-related. Figure 3-1 shows how.

Managing the Network's Center

When agility is viewed through a network lens, it becomes apparent that collaboration is never equally distributed. We typically see that 20%–35% of valuable collaborations come from only 3%–5% of employees. Through no fault of their own, these people become overly relied upon and tend to slow group responsiveness, despite working to their wits' end. They are more likely to burn out and leave the company, creating network gaps, which then become another barrier to agility. Senior leaders need to consider where overload on the network's center might preclude agile collaboration and:

- Encourage overwhelmed employees to redistribute collaborative work in conjunction with their managers. Groundbreaking work from the Institute for

FIGURE 3-1

To manage collaboration, pay attention to four points of execution

Ask yourself if you're identifying networks' centers, leveraging their edges, bringing silos together, and making external connections.

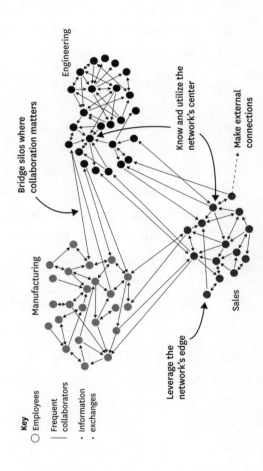

Bridge silos where collaboration matters

Engineering

Know and utilize the network's center

Make external connections

Manufacturing

Key

○ Employees

| Frequent collaborators

▴ Information
▸ exchanges

Leverage the network's edge

Sales

Source: Alia Crocker et al.

Corporate Productivity found that acknowledging and shifting collaborative demands in this way is a practice that's three times more likely to be found in high-performing organizations than in those with lower performance.[1]

- Understand how employees have ended up in the center—and if it is a result of formal position or personal characteristics, then take the corrective actions necessary to reduce overload. For example, simple shifts in a few behaviors can yield as much as 18%–24% more time for collaboration.[2] Such behaviors include managing meetings more efficiently, creating an effective climate of email use, blocking time in calendars for reflective work, negotiating role demands, and avoiding triggers that lead us all to jump in on projects or meetings when we shouldn't, to name just a few.

- Map the interdependencies between different teams where your central players contribute, in order to understand and plan for potential risks. When a star sits at the center of multiple projects, a surprise shock in one team can create nasty ripples well beyond the jolted team. Be sure team leaders have a backup plan to cover these emergencies.

Engaging the Network's Fringe Players

Agility requires the integration of different capabilities and perspectives to understand VUCA issues and figure out what kinds of experts are needed to tackle them. But those who see the world differently or who are new to a group often languish at the network edges. Whereas those in the center may be overrelied on, those on the fringes are often not tapped in a way that allows for agile collaboration. For example, our research shows that it can take three to five years for a newcomer to replicate the connectivity of a high performer.[3] Few organizations provide such luxury of time, however: our research also shows that if an experienced hire doesn't get integrated into substantive projects *within the first year*, they are seriously at risk of leaving before they reach the three-year mark.

Getting others to trust fringe employees is essential for drawing them into agile collaboration. Their competence isn't usually in question if you have rigorous hiring and merit-based promotion processes; the trick is getting others to trust their motives ("Will he take undue credit?" or "Will she walk away with my clients?") if few colleagues can vouch for their character. Senior management can help by taking the following actions:

- Create a "hidden gems" program to help unearth high-potential but overlooked experts who could take some of the burden off overworked central players. Role model this behavior by, for example, assigning an up-and-comer to co-lead a high-status initiative.

- Help those on the fringe to create "pull" for their work. Instead of pushing expertise on others across the network, these employees need to be seen as a strategic resource to be pulled into opportunities. This is done by identifying mutual value and matching capabilities from the fringe to needs across the network.

- Pair newcomers and network influencers through staffing or mentoring. This simple practice triples newcomer connectivity compared to those who do not get this experience.

- Create inclusive and trusting environments to facilitate agile collaboration. A culture of fear exists when employees do not feel safe to come forward with ideas, and those on the fringe may be less confident about contributing. High-performing organizations are 2.5 times more likely to facilitate an environment of safe communication.[4]

Bridging Select Silos

Every organization we studied struggled with silos across functions, expertise, geography, level, and cultures—whether occupational or national. The network lens can help uncover specific points that, if crossed, could yield agility benefits, rather than inefficiently bridging all silos. Often, this means connecting people across units or geographies doing similar work to yield benefits of scale or identifying points where integrating different perspectives yields agile innovation. This type of multidisciplinary collaboration produces higher revenues and profits because it tackles higher-value problems. Motivating experts to engage in agile collaboration requires them not only to identify and appreciate knowledge from other silos but also to be willing to give up some control and autonomy over a project's direction. Senior leaders can help motivate experts with the following actions:

- Set specific goals and reward agile collaboration. Our research found that, compared to lower-performing organizations, high-performance organizations are three to five times more likely to reward collaboration,[5] motivating employees to move beyond silos. Our studies of firms that use peer feedback to effectively identify and celebrate agile collaborators show that these bottom-up processes often uncover excellent people whom the formal performance reviews might otherwise overlook.

- **Use data and analytics to understand where silos exist, in order to unlock possible agile collaboration.** In one study, we found discrepancies in connections between headquarters and affiliates, and poor collaboration between engineering and sales. This insight produced the business case for holding brainstorming sessions to build connections and improve communication. A data-driven approach is not only more accurate and less biased than relying on individuals' perceptions, but also more convincingly demonstrates the quantifiable upside for agile collaboration.

- **Identify experts scattered across silos and key cross-points in the firm for agile collaboration.** Set up communities of practice or business development initiatives to help share expertise or resources. For example, many business service firms are prompting professionals who serve customers in similar industries such as insurance or biotech to meet informally and share sector insights and leads. The well-connected professionals act as bridges to and from silos. Some firms have successfully tasked high-potential employees with tracking the evolving expertise in adjacent departments, which has to be a dynamic process, definitely not a knowledge database. These employees should be recognized for identifying opportunities to use cross-silo knowledge. Exchange programs or rotational programs can help here, too.

Spanning External Boundaries

Agility thrives when employees understand their organization within the broader ecosystem and continually scan for market developments that pose either threats or opportunities. Doing so requires dynamic knowledge of external bodies such as competitors, customers, regulators, and expertise communities or associations. Those who span the boundary between internal and external actors can solve problems in unique ways, because they can access knowledge from these different worlds. They can also facilitate agile collaboration by efficiently integrating disparate viewpoints and creating multistakeholder solutions, but they need to be properly empowered, managed, and resourced in order to do so. Senior managers can facilitate this by doing the following:

- **Identify and enlist boundary spanners to help tackle vexing problems.** People who connect the organization with its ecosystem can propose plans that can be feasibly implemented, since they have access to the shortest informational paths in the network and legitimacy in the broader environmental context.

- **Nurture relationships and promote the exchange of information by organizing forums or special events that convene key players from across the ecosystem.** This approach helps to create more people in your organization who are capable of functioning as bridges to external parties, and it provides insights on pain points and opportunities in the ecosystem.

- **Promote connectivity to key external stakeholders.** High-performing organizations are 2.5 times more likely to encourage interaction with external stakeholders such as clients, suppliers, regulatory bodies, or professional associations.[6] Senior managers should require employees who are well connected internally to work on external connections, or suggest that those who are well connected externally mentor junior employees in networking to ensure boundary spanning.

Managing these collaborative players as part of a network can help organizations be more agile. Although agile collaboration requires continual reassessment of complex problems, it is possible for firms to combine and recombine essential expertise from across points in the network to address VUCA issues. By steadily nurturing agile collaboration, senior management can more effectively and more efficiently access the necessary depth of expertise of key collaborators within the organization.

TAKEAWAYS

Collaboration is central to agility, yet most work is done by combinations of colleagues that don't report up the same formal ladder or share standard processes. To enjoy true benefits of scale, networks drawn from employees across core work and temporary teams should nurture themselves by:

✓ Mapping interdependencies between teams to understand and plan for potential risks

✓ Drawing in fringe players by creating a "hidden gems" program to help unearth high-potential but overlooked experts; matching capabilities to needs across the network; pairing newcomers and network influencers through staffing or mentoring; and creating inclusive and trusting environments

✓ Connecting people doing similar work by setting specific goals and rewarding collaboration; using data and analytics to understand where silos exist; and establishing communities of practice to share expertise and resources

✓ Staying vigilant about overload, considering where it might hinder collaboration and redistributing work accordingly

✓ Understanding your organization within the broader ecosystem and scanning for market developments that pose threats or opportunities

NOTES

1. Institute for Corporate Productivity, "Purposeful Collaboration: The Essential Components of Collaborative Cultures," 2017, http://go.i4cp.com/purposefulcollaboration.pdf.

2. Network Assessments, "Understanding Collaborative Overload," 2018, https://www.networkassessments.org/collaborative -overload/.

3. Connected Commons, "Connect and Adapt—Improving Retention and Engagement in First Five Years," video, 2019, https://

connectedcommons.com/connect-and-adapt-improving-retention
-and-engagement-in-first-five-years-video/.

4. Institute for Corporate Productivity, "Purposeful Collaboration: The Essential Components of Collaborative Cultures."

5. Ibid.

6. Ibid.

Adapted from content posted on hbr.org, May 15, 2018 (product #H04BXH).

HOW NEXTDOOR ADDRESSED RACIAL PROFILING ON ITS PLATFORM

by Phil Simon

O
n March 3, 2015, hyperlocal social network Nextdoor announced that it had raised $110 million in venture capital. The deal valued the company at more than $1 billion—revered, unicorn status. It had to be a giddy moment for CEO Nirav Tolia and cofounders David Wiesen, Prakash Janakiraman, and Sarah Leary.

But just three weeks later, all of that celebrating must have seemed like a distant memory.

The news site Fusion ran an article explaining how Nextdoor "is becoming a home for racial profiling."[1] Reporter Pendarvis Harshaw detailed how presumably white members were using Nextdoor's crime and safety forum to report "suspicious" activities by African Americans and Latinos. Jennifer Medina of the *New York Times* followed up, reporting that "as Nextdoor has grown, users have complained that it has become a magnet for racial profiling, leading African-American and Latino residents to be seen as suspects in their own neighborhoods."[2]

As I discuss in my book *Analytics: The Agile Way*, how Nextdoor responded illustrates not only the importance of reacting quickly in a crisis but the usefulness of a data-driven, agile approach.

The Response

Agile teams benefit from different perspectives, skills, and expertise, so the cofounders assembled a small, diverse team to tackle the issue. Members included product head Maryam Mohit, communications director Kelsey Grady, a product manager, a designer, a data scientist, and later a software engineer.

As for the data, much of Nextdoor's data here was unstructured text. Especially at first, this sort of data doesn't lend itself to the type of easy analysis that its structured equivalent does. This goes double when trying to deal with a thorny issue such as racial profiling. Five employees were assigned to read through thousands of user posts.

The outcome was a three-pronged solution: diversity training for Nextdoor's neighborhood operations team; an update to Nextdoor's community guidelines and an accompanying blog post; and a redesign of the app. This last step proved to be the thorniest.

Nextdoor had long allowed people to flag inappropriate posts, by either content or location. For instance, commercial posts didn't belong in noncommercial areas of the site. Nextdoor realized that a binary (re: flagged or not flagged) was no longer sufficient. Its first attempt at fixing the problem was simply to add a *report racial profiling* button. But many users didn't understand the new feature. "Nextdoor members began reporting all kinds of unrelated slights as racial profiling. 'Somebody reported her neighbor for writing mean things about pit bulls,' Mohit recall[ed]."[3]

The team responded by developing six different variants of its app and testing them. Doing so helped the company answer key questions such as:

- If the app alerted users about the potential for racial bias before they posted, would it change user behavior?

- Characterizing a person isn't easy. How does an application prompt its users for descriptions of others that are full and fair, rather than based exclusively on race?

- In describing a suspicious person, how many attributes are enough? Which specific attributes are more important than others?

Using lean methods, the team conducted a series of A/B tests. Blessed with a sufficiently large user base, Nextdoor ran experiments to determine the right answers to these questions. For instance, consider two groups of 25,000 users divided into cohorts (A and B). Each group would see one version of the Nextdoor app with slight but important differences in question wording, order, required fields, and the like.

Over the course of three months, Nextdoor's different permutations made clear that certain versions of the app worked far better than others. And by August 2015, the team was ready to launch a new posting protocol in its crime and safety section. Users who mentioned race when posting to "Crime & Safety" forums were prompted to provide additional information, such as hair, clothing, and shoes.

The Results

Simply adding additional details and a little bit of user friction did not eliminate posts by insensitive people or racist users with axes to grind. But by taking a data-oriented and agile approach to design, the company reported it had reduced racial profiling by 75%.

Nextdoor was able to stem the bleeding in a relatively short period of time. A different organization would have announced plans to "study the problem" as it continued unabated. Nextdoor took a different approach, and the results speak for themselves.

TAKEAWAYS

When multiple reports emerged with details of how presumably white members were using Nextdoor's crime and safety forum to report "suspicious" activities by African Americans and Latinos, the company responded with the conventional approaches of more diversity training and updates to its community guidelines. But Nextdoor went one step further by also using agile to explore potential app feature solutions. The quick response this approach afforded Nextdoor provides a great example of agile as a solution to even the thorniest problems.

✓ Nextdoor already had a function for folks to flag inappropriate posts, but it realized the binary (flagged/not flagged) was no longer sufficient.

✓ Its team developed six variants of its app and conducted a series of A/B tests with users to answer key questions such as "How can an app prompt users for descriptions of others that are full and fair?" and "How many attributes are enough?" to describe a suspicious person.

✓ After three months, Nextdoor had enough data to demonstrate that certain versions of the app worked better than others.

✓ Just five months after the initial news reports, Nextdoor was ready to launch a new posting protocol in its crime and safety section that reduced racial profiling by 75%.

NOTES

1. Pendarvis Harshaw, "Nextdoor, the Social Network for Neighbors, Is Becoming a Home for Racial Profiling," Splinter, March 24, 2015, https://splinternews.com/nextdoor-the-social -network-for-neighbors-is-becoming-1793846596.

2. Jennifer Medina, "Website Meant to Connect Neighbors Hears Complaints of Racial Profiling," *New York Times*, May 18, 2016, https://www.nytimes.com/2016/05/19/us/website-nextdoor-hears -racial-profiling-complaints.html?mtrref=undefined&gwh=D02E4 A7AEBE5A737D229D57AF463DF05&gwt=pay&_r=0.

3. Jessi Hempel, "For Nextdoor, Eliminating Racism Is No Quick Fix," *Wired*, February 16, 2017, https://www.wired.com/2017/02/for -nextdoor-eliminating-racism-is-no-quick-fix/#.byvblyn7y.

Adapted from content posted on hbr.org, May 11, 2018 (product #H04BFP).

5

HR GOES AGILE

by Peter Cappelli and Anna Tavis

Agile isn't just for tech anymore. It's been working its way into other areas and functions, from product development to manufacturing to marketing—and now it's transforming how organizations hire, develop, and manage their people.

You could say HR is going "agile lite," applying the general principles without adopting all the tools and protocols from the tech world. It's a move away from a rules- and planning-based approach toward a simpler and faster model driven by feedback from participants. This new paradigm has really taken off in the area of performance management. (In a 2017 Deloitte survey, 79% of global executives rated agile performance management as a high organizational priority.) But other HR processes are starting to change too.

In many companies that's happening gradually, almost organically, as a spillover from IT, where more than 90% of organizations already use agile practices. At the Bank of Montreal (BMO), for example, the shift began as tech employees joined cross-functional product-development teams to make the bank more customer focused. The business side has learned agile principles from IT colleagues, and IT has learned about customer needs from the business. One result is that BMO now thinks about performance management in terms of teams, not just individuals. Elsewhere the move to agile HR has been faster and more deliberate. GE is a prime example. Seen for many years as a paragon of management through control systems, it switched to FastWorks, a lean approach that cuts back on top-down financial controls and empowers teams to manage projects as needs evolve.

The changes in HR have been a long time coming. After World War II, when manufacturing dominated the industrial landscape, planning was at the heart of human resources: Companies recruited lifers, gave them rotational assignments to support their development, groomed them years in advance to take on bigger and bigger roles, and tied their raises directly to each incremental move up the ladder. The bureaucracy was the point: Organizations wanted their talent practices to be rules based and internally consistent so that they could reliably meet five-year (and sometimes fifteen-year) plans. That made sense. Every other aspect of companies, from core businesses to administrative functions, took the long view in their goal setting, budgeting, and operations. HR reflected and supported what they were doing.

By the 1990s, as business became less predictable and companies needed to acquire new skills fast, that traditional approach began to bend—but it didn't quite break. Lateral hiring from the outside—to get more flexibility—replaced a good deal of the internal development and promotions. "Broadband" compensation gave managers greater latitude to reward people for growth and achievement within roles. For the most part, though, the old model persisted. Like other functions, HR was still built around the long term. Workforce and succession planning carried on, even though changes in the economy and in the business often rendered those plans irrelevant. Annual appraisals continued, despite almost universal dissatisfaction with them.

Now we're seeing a more sweeping transformation. Why is this the moment for it? Because rapid innovation has become a strategic imperative for most companies, not just a subset. To get it, businesses have looked to Silicon Valley and to software companies in particular, emulating their agile practices for managing projects. So top-down planning models are giving way to nimbler, user-driven methods that are better suited for adapting in the near term, such as rapid prototyping, iterative feedback, team-based decisions, and task-centered "sprints." As BMO's chief transformation officer, Lynn Roger, puts it, "Speed is the new business currency."

With the business justification for the old HR systems gone and the agile playbook available to copy, people management is finally getting its long-awaited overhaul too. In this article we'll illustrate some of the profound changes companies are making in their talent practices and describe the challenges they face in their transition to agile HR.

Where We're Seeing the Biggest Changes

Because HR touches every aspect—and every employee— of an organization, its agile transformation may be even more extensive (and more difficult) than the changes in other functions. Companies are redesigning their talent practices in the following areas:

Performance appraisals

When businesses adopted agile methods in their core operations, they dropped the charade of trying to plan a year or more in advance how projects would go and when they would end. So in many cases the first traditional HR practice to go was the annual performance review, along with employee goals that "cascaded" down from business and unit objectives each year. As individuals worked on shorter-term projects of various lengths, often run by different leaders and organized around teams, the notion that performance feedback would come once a year, from one boss, made little sense. They needed more of it, more often, from more people.

An early-days CEB survey suggested that people actually got *less* feedback and support when their employers dropped annual reviews. However, that's because many companies put nothing in their place. Managers felt no pressing need to adopt a new feedback model and shifted their attention to other priorities. But dropping appraisals without a plan to fill the void was of course a recipe for failure.

Since learning that hard lesson, many organizations have switched to frequent performance assessments, often conducted project by project. This change has spread to a number of industries, including retail (Gap), big pharma (Pfizer), insurance (Cigna), investing (OppenheimerFunds), consumer products (P&G), and accounting (all Big Four firms). It is most famous at GE, across the firm's range of businesses, and at IBM. Overall, the focus is on delivering more-immediate feedback throughout the year so that teams can become nimbler, "course-correct" mistakes, improve performance, and learn through iteration—all key agile principles.

In user-centered fashion, managers and employees have had a hand in shaping, testing, and refining new processes. For instance, Johnson & Johnson offered its businesses the chance to participate in an experiment: They could try out a new continual-feedback process, using a customized app with which employees, peers, and bosses could exchange comments in real time.

The new process was an attempt to move away from J&J's event-driven "five conversations" framework (which focused on goal setting, career discussion, a midyear performance review, a year-end appraisal, and a compensation review) and toward a model of ongoing dialogue. Those who tried it were asked to share how well everything worked, what the bugs were, and so on. The experiment lasted three months. At first only 20% of the managers in the pilot actively participated. The inertia from prior years of annual appraisals was hard to overcome. But then the company used training to show managers what good feedback could look like and designated "change champions" to model the desired behaviors on their teams. By the end of the three months, 46% of managers in the pilot group had joined in, exchanging 3,000 pieces of feedback. (See the sidebar "Why Intuit's Transition to Agile Almost Stalled Out.")

Why Intuit's Transition to Agile Almost Stalled Out

The financial services division at Intuit began shifting to agile in 2009—but four years went by before that became standard operating procedure across the company.

What took so long? Leaders started with a "waterfall" approach to change management, because that's what they knew best. It didn't work. Spotty support from middle management, part-time commitments to the team leading the transformation, scarce administrative resources, and an extended planning cycle all put a big drag on the rollout.

Before agile could gain traction throughout the organization, the transition team needed to take an agile approach to *becoming* agile and managing the change. Looking back, Joumana Youssef, one of Intuit's strategic-change leaders, identifies several critical discoveries that changed the course—and the speed—of the transformation:

- Focus on early adopters. Don't waste time trying to convert naysayers.

(continued)

- Form "triple-S" (small, stable, self-managed) teams, give them ownership of their work, and hold them accountable for their commitments.

- Quickly train leaders at all levels in agile methods. Agile teams need to be fully supported to self-manage.

- Expect that changing frontline and middle management will be hard, because people in those roles need time to acclimate to "servant leadership," which is primarily about coaching and supporting employees rather than monitoring them.

- Stay the course. Even though agile change is faster than a waterfall approach, shifting your organization's mind-set takes persistence.

Regeneron Pharmaceuticals, a fast-growing biotech company, is going even further with its appraisals overhaul. Michelle Weitzman-Garcia, Regeneron's head of workforce development, argued that the performance of the scientists working on drug development, the product supply group, the field sales force, and the corporate functions should not be measured on the same cycle or in the same way. She observed that these employee groups needed varying feedback and that they even operated on different calendars.

So the company created four distinct appraisal processes, tailored to the various groups' needs. The research scientists and postdocs, for example, crave metrics and are keen on assessing competencies, so they meet with managers twice a year for competency evaluations and milestones reviews. Customer-facing groups include feedback from clients and customers in their assessments. Although having to manage four separate processes adds complexity, they all reinforce the new norm of continual feedback. And Weitzman-Garcia says the benefits to the organization far outweigh the costs to HR.

Coaching

The companies that most effectively adopt agile talent practices invest in sharpening managers' coaching skills. Supervisors at Cigna go through "coach" training designed for busy managers: It's broken into weekly 90-minute videos that can be viewed as people have time. The supervisors also engage in learning sessions, which, like "learning sprints" in agile project management, are brief and spread out to allow individuals to reflect and test-drive new skills on the job. Peer-to-peer feedback is incorporated in Cigna's manager training too: Colleagues form learning cohorts to share ideas and tactics. They're having the kinds of conversations companies want supervisors to have with their direct reports, but they feel freer to share mistakes with one another, without the fear of "evaluation" hanging over their heads.

DigitalOcean, a New York–based startup focused on software as a service (SaaS) infrastructure, engages a full-time professional coach on-site to help all managers give better feedback to employees and, more broadly, to develop internal coaching capabilities. The idea is that once one experiences good coaching, one becomes a better coach. Not everyone is expected to become a great coach—those in the company who prefer coding to coaching can advance along a technical career track—but coaching skills are considered central to a managerial career.

P&G, too, is intent on making managers better coaches. That's part of a larger effort to rebuild training and development for supervisors and enhance their role in the organization. By simplifying the performance review process, separating evaluation from development discussions, and eliminating talent calibration sessions (the arbitrary horse trading between supervisors that often comes with a subjective and politicized ranking model),

P&G has freed up a lot of time to devote to employees' growth. But getting supervisors to move from judging employees to coaching them in their day-to-day work has been a challenge in P&G's tradition-rich culture. So the company has invested heavily in training supervisors on topics such as how to establish employees' priorities and goals, how to provide feedback about contributions, and how to align employees' career aspirations with business needs and learning and development plans. The bet is that building employees' capabilities and relationships with supervisors will increase engagement and therefore help the company innovate and move faster. Even though the jury is still out on the companywide culture shift, P&G is already reporting improvements in these areas, at all levels of management.

Teams

Traditional HR focused on individuals—their goals, their performance, their needs. But now that so many companies are organizing their work project by project, their management and talent systems are becoming more team focused. Groups are creating, executing, and revising their goals and tasks with scrums—at the team level, in the moment, to adapt quickly to new information as it comes in. ("Scrum" may be the best-known term in the agile lexicon. It comes from rugby, where players pack tightly together to restart play.) They are also taking it upon themselves to track their own progress, identify obstacles, assess their leadership, and generate insights about how to improve performance.

In that context, organizations must learn to contend with:

Multidirectional feedback. Peer feedback is essential to course corrections and employee development in an agile environment, because team members know better than anyone else what each person is contributing. It's rarely a formal process, and comments are generally directed to the employee, not the supervisor. That keeps input constructive and prevents the undermining of colleagues that sometimes occurs in hypercompetitive workplaces.

But some executives believe that peer feedback should have an impact on performance evaluations. Diane Gherson, IBM's head of HR, explains that "the relationships between managers and employees change in the context of a network [the collection of projects across which employees work]." Because an agile environment makes it practically impossible to "monitor" performance in the old sense, managers at IBM solicit input from others to help them identify and address issues early on. Unless it's sensitive, that input is shared in the team's daily stand-up meetings and captured in an app. Employees may choose whether to include managers and others in their comments to peers. The risk of cutthroat behavior is mitigated by the fact that peer comments to the supervisor also go to the team. Anyone trying to undercut colleagues will be exposed.

In agile organizations, "upward" feedback from employees to team leaders and supervisors is highly valued too. The Mitre Corporation's not-for-profit research centers have taken steps to encourage it, but they're finding that this requires concentrated effort. They started with periodic confidential employee surveys and focus groups to discover which issues people wanted to discuss with their managers. HR then distilled that data for supervisors to inform their conversations with direct reports. However, employees were initially hesitant to provide upward feedback—even though it was anonymous and was used for development purposes only—because they weren't accustomed to voicing their thoughts about what management was doing.

Mitre also learned that the most critical factor in getting subordinates to be candid was having managers explicitly say that they wanted and appreciated comments. Otherwise people might worry, reasonably, that their leaders weren't really open to feedback and ready to apply it. As with any employee survey, soliciting upward feedback and not acting on it has a diminishing effect on participation; it erodes the hard-earned trust between employees and their managers. When Mitre's new performance-management and feedback process began, the CEO acknowledged that the research centers would need to iterate and make improvements. A revised system for upward feedback will roll out this year.

Because feedback flows in all directions on teams, many companies use technology to manage the sheer volume of it. Apps allow supervisors, coworkers, and clients to give one another immediate feedback from wherever they are. Crucially, supervisors can download all the comments later on, when it's time to do evaluations. In some apps, employees and supervisors can score progress on goals; at least one helps managers analyze conversations on project management platforms like Slack to provide feedback on collaboration. Cisco uses proprietary technology to collect weekly raw data, or "bread crumbs," from employees about their peers' performance. Such tools enable managers to see fluctuations in individual performance over time, even within teams. The apps don't provide an official record of performance, of course, and employees may want to discuss problems face-to-face to avoid having them recorded in a file that can be downloaded. We know that companies recognize and reward improvement as well as actual performance, however, so hiding problems may not always pay off for employees.

Frontline decision rights. The fundamental shift toward teams has also affected decision rights: Organizations are pushing them down to the front lines, equipping and empowering employees to operate more independently. But that's a huge behavioral change, and people need support to pull it off. Let's return to the Bank of Montreal example to illustrate how it can work. When BMO introduced agile teams to design some new customer services, senior leaders weren't quite ready to give up control, and the people under them were not used to taking it. So the bank embedded agile coaches in business teams. They began by putting everyone, including high-level executives, through "retrospectives"—regular reflection and feedback sessions held after each iteration. These are the agile version of after-action reviews; their purpose is to keep improving processes. Because the retrospectives quickly identified concrete successes, failures, and root causes, senior leaders at BMO immediately recognized their value, which helped them get on board with agile generally and loosen their grip on decision making.

Complex team dynamics. Finally, since the supervisor's role has moved away from just managing individuals and toward the much more complicated task of promoting productive, healthy team dynamics, people often need help with that, too. Cisco's special Team Intelligence unit provides that kind of support. It's charged with identifying the company's best-performing teams, analyzing how they operate, and helping other teams learn how to become more like them. It uses an enterprise-wide platform called Team Space, which tracks data on team projects, needs, and achievements to both measure and improve what teams are doing within units and across the company.

Compensation

Pay is changing as well. A simple adaptation to agile work, seen in retail companies such as Macy's, is to use spot bonuses to recognize contributions when they happen rather than rely solely on end-of-year salary increases. Research and practice have shown that compensation works best as a motivator when it comes as soon as possible after the desired behavior. Instant rewards reinforce instant feedback in a powerful way. Annual merit-based raises are less effective, because too much time goes by.

Patagonia has actually eliminated annual raises for its knowledge workers. Instead the company adjusts wages for each job much more frequently, according to research on where market rates are going. Increases can also be allocated when employees take on more-difficult projects or go above and beyond in other ways. The company retains a budget for the top 1% of individual contributors, and supervisors can make a case for any contribution that merits that designation, including contributions to teams.

Compensation is also being used to reinforce agile values such as learning and knowledge sharing. In the startup world, for instance, the online clothing-rental company Rent the Runway dropped separate bonuses, rolling the money into base pay. CEO Jennifer Hyman reports that the bonus program was getting in the way of honest peer feedback. Employees weren't sharing constructive criticism, knowing it could have negative financial consequences for their colleagues. The new system prevents that problem by "untangling the two," Hyman says.

DigitalOcean redesigned its rewards to promote equitable treatment of employees and a culture of collaboration. Salary adjustments now happen twice a year to respond to changes in the outside labor market and in jobs and performance. More important, DigitalOcean has closed gaps in pay for equivalent work. It's deliberately heading off internal rivalry, painfully aware of the problems in hypercompetitive cultures (think Microsoft and Amazon). To personalize compensation, the firm maps where people are having impact in their roles and where they need to grow and develop. The data on individuals' impact on the business is a key factor in discussions about pay. Negotiating to raise your own salary is fiercely discouraged. And only the top 1% of achievement is rewarded financially; otherwise, there is no merit-pay process. All employees are eligible for bonuses, which are based on company performance rather than individual contributions. To further support collaboration, DigitalOcean is diversifying its portfolio of rewards to include nonfinancial, meaningful gifts, such as a Kindle loaded with the CEO's "best books" picks.

How does DigitalOcean motivate people to perform their best without inflated financial rewards? Matt Hoffman, its vice president of people, says it focuses on creating a culture that inspires purpose and creativity. So far that seems to be working. The latest engagement survey, via Culture Amp, ranks DigitalOcean 17 points above the industry benchmark in satisfaction with compensation.

Recruiting

With the improvements in the economy since the Great Recession, recruiting and hiring have become more urgent—and more agile. To scale up quickly in 2015, GE's new digital division pioneered some interesting recruiting experiments. For instance, a cross-functional team works together on all hiring requisitions. A "head count manager" represents the interests of internal stakeholders who want their positions filled quickly and appropriately. Hiring managers rotate on and off the team, depending on whether they're currently hiring, and a scrum master oversees the process.

To keep things moving, the team focuses on vacancies that have cleared all the hurdles—no req's get started if debate is still ongoing about the desired attributes of candidates. Openings are ranked, and the team concentrates on the top-priority hires until they are completed. It works on several hires at once so that members can share information about candidates who may fit better in other roles. The team keeps track of its cycle time for filling positions and monitors all open requisitions on a kanban board to identify bottlenecks and blocked processes. IBM now takes a similar approach to recruitment.

Companies are also relying more heavily on technology to find and track candidates who are well suited to an agile work environment. GE, IBM, and Cisco are working with the vendor Ascendify to create software that does just this. The IT recruiting company HackerRank offers an online tool for the same purpose.

Learning and development

Like hiring, L&D had to change to bring new skills into organizations more quickly. Most companies already have a suite of online learning modules that employees can access on demand. Although helpful for those who have clearly defined needs, this is a bit like giving a student the key to a library and telling her to figure out what she must know and then learn it. Newer approaches use data analysis to identify the skills required for particular jobs and for advancement and then suggest to individual employees what kinds of training and future jobs make sense for them, given their experience and interests.

IBM uses artificial intelligence to generate such advice, starting with employees' profiles, which include prior and current roles, expected career trajectory, and training programs completed. The company has also created special training for agile environments—using, for example, animated simulations built around a series of "personas" to illustrate useful behaviors, such as offering constructive criticism. (See the sidebar "What HR Can Learn from Tech.")

Traditionally, L&D has included succession planning—the epitome of top-down, long-range thinking, whereby individuals are picked years in advance to take on the most crucial leadership roles, usually in the hope that they will develop certain capabilities on schedule. The world often fails to cooperate with those plans, though. Companies routinely find that by the time senior leadership positions open up, their needs have changed. The most common solution is to ignore the plan and start a search from scratch. But organizations often continue doing long-term succession planning anyway. (About half of large companies have a plan to develop successors for the top job.) Pepsi is one company taking a simple step away from this model by shortening the time frame. It provides brief quarterly updates on

What HR Can Learn from Tech

The agile pioneers in the tech world are years ahead of everyone else in adopting the methodology at scale. So who better to provide guidance as managers and HR leaders grapple with how to apply agile talent practices throughout their organizations? In a recent survey, thousands of software developers across many countries and industries identified their biggest obstacles in scaling and the ways they got past them.

(continued)

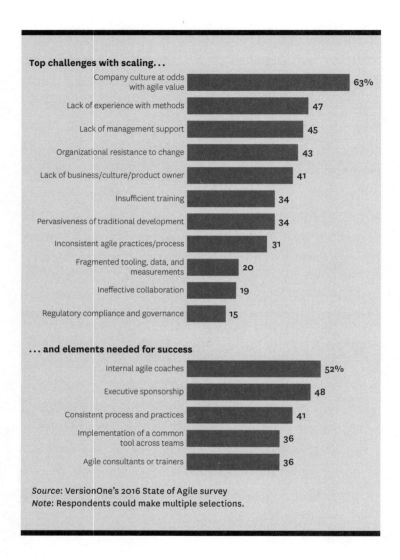

Top challenges with scaling...

Company culture at odds with agile value	63%
Lack of experience with methods	47
Lack of management support	45
Organizational resistance to change	43
Lack of business/culture/product owner	41
Insufficient training	34
Pervasiveness of traditional development	34
Inconsistent agile practices/process	31
Fragmented tooling, data, and measurements	20
Ineffective collaboration	19
Regulatory compliance and governance	15

... and elements needed for success

Internal agile coaches	52%
Executive sponsorship	48
Consistent process and practices	41
Implementation of a common tool across teams	36
Agile consultants or trainers	36

Source: VersionOne's 2016 State of Agile survey
Note: Respondents could make multiple selections.

the development of possible successors—in contrast to the usual annual updates—and delays appointments so that they happen closer to when successors are likely to step into their roles.

Ongoing Challenges

To be sure, not every organization or group is in hot pursuit of rapid innovation. Some jobs must remain largely rules based. (Consider the work that accountants, nuclear control-room operators, and surgeons do.) In such cases agile talent practices may not make sense.

And even when they're appropriate, they may meet resistance—especially within HR. A lot of processes have to change for an organization to move away from a planning-based "waterfall" model (which is linear rather than flexible and adaptive), and some of them are hardwired into information systems, job titles, and so forth. The move toward cloud-based IT, which is happening independently, has made it easier to adopt app-based tools. But people issues remain a sticking point. Many HR tasks, such as traditional approaches to recruitment, onboarding, and program coordination, will become obsolete, as will expertise in those areas.

Meanwhile, new tasks are being created. Helping supervisors replace judging with coaching is a big challenge not just in terms of skills but also because it undercuts their status and formal authority. Shifting the focus of management from individuals to teams may be even more difficult, because team dynamics can be a black box to those who are still struggling to understand how to coach individuals. The big question is whether companies can help managers take all this on and see the value in it.

The HR function will also require reskilling. It will need more expertise in IT support—especially given all the performance data generated by the new apps—and deeper knowledge about teams and hands-on supervision. HR has not had to change in recent decades nearly as much as have the line operations it supports. But now the pressure is on, and it's coming from the operating level, which makes it much harder to cling to old talent practices.

Agile is extending its reach beyond tech and project management into the most people-centered realm of human resources. It can transform how your organization hires, develops, and manages its people in these key areas:

- ✓ Performance appraisals: Frequent performance assessments, often conducted project by project, help employees correct course, improve performance, and learn through iteration.

- ✓ Coaching: Video trainings, brief learning sessions that allow employees to test-drive new skills on the job, and peer-to-peer feedback remove the fear of evaluation and create a culture where learning from mistakes is the norm.

- ✓ Teams: Collaboration is improved by using multi-directional feedback, shifting decision rights to the front line, and promoting productive and healthy team dynamics.

- ✓ Compensation: Spot bonuses to reward and reinforce instant feedback replace annual salary reviews and calendar-based bonuses, and salary reviews and adjustments become more responsive to performance and outside labor market changes.

- ✓ Recruiting: A cross-functional team makes all hires, focuses on top-priority vacancies, and works on several hires at once so members can share information about candidates who may fit better in other roles.

✓ Learning and development: Data analysis identifies the skills required for specific jobs and advancement, so training and future roles for individuals can be personalized.

Reprinted from Harvard Business Review, *March–April 2018 (product #R1802B).*

HOW TO MAKE AGILE WORK FOR THE C-SUITE

by Eric Garton and Andy Noble

Many companies are attempting a radical—and often rapid—shift from hierarchical structures to more agile environments, in order to operate at the speed required by today's competitive marketplace. Companies like ANZ, the Australian-based banking giant, have made explicit commitments to adopt agile principles, while others like Zappos are on the bleeding edge of organizational transformation. Many stopping points exist along the continuum from hierarchy to holacracy. To successfully transform to a more agile enterprise, companies must make conscious choices about where and how to become agile. They have to decide where to adopt agile principles and mindsets, where to use agile problem-solving methodologies to dynamically address strategic and organizational challenges, and where to more formally deploy the full agile model, including self-managed teams.

At Bain & Company, we do not believe that companies should try to use agile methods everywhere. In many functional areas, such as plant maintenance, purchasing, sales calls, or accounting, more traditional structures and processes likely will deliver lower-cost, more repeatable outcomes and more scalable organizations. Sorting through every function and every part of your company's operating model to determine which parts of the agile playbook to adopt requires some deep thinking. It also means you have to figure out how to make the agile and traditional parts of your organization effectively operate with one another. This takes time.

There is, however, a no-regrets first move available to the leaders of organizations that are working through a complicated transition from a traditional to an agile enterprise, and that is to become agile at the top. Senior leadership teams that embrace agile do a few things differently. Based on our experience working with these teams, we recommend senior teams do the following if they want to become more agile.

Treat your enterprise priorities as a managed backlog

At the enterprise level, think of all of your corporate initiatives as a backlog, just as software developers think of future product features as a backlog. See your leadership team as an agile scrum that prioritizes the backlog based on importance, then tackles them in sequence until completed. Reprioritize your enterprise backlog when new initiatives are added. This helps maintain focus and velocity while stopping initiative proliferation. Systematic Inc., a 525-employee software company, began applying agile methodologies in 2005. As they spread to all its software development teams, Michael Holm, the company's CEO and cofounder, began to worry that his leadership team was hindering progress. So in 2010, Holm decided to run his nine-member executive group as an agile team. The group started by meeting every Monday for an hour or two but found the pace of decision making too slow. So it began having daily 20-minute stand-ups at 8:40 a.m. to discuss what members had done the day before, what they would do that day, and where they needed help.

Executive teams looking to adopt this practice need to focus on fewer things and move from a calendar-based planning process to continuous issue-based planning. When Steve Jobs was running Apple, one of his greatest strengths was ruthlessly focusing the company on its most critical priorities. As documented by Walter Isaacson, "After he righted the company, Jobs began taking his 'top 100' people on a retreat each year. On the last day, he would stand in front of a whiteboard and ask, 'What are the 10 things we should be doing next?' People would fight to get their suggestions on the list. Jobs would write them down—and then cross off the ones he decreed dumb. After much jockeying, the group would come up with a list of 10. Then Jobs would slash the bottom seven and announce, 'We can only do three.'"

And it's not just executive focus that needs to change. The traditional annual strategic planning cycle must be supplemented with real-time, issue-based planning so resources can be allocated more dynamically. Strategy, competitor actions, and timely responses do not fit neatly into a fixed calendar. Companies like Textron and Cardinal Health began moving toward a more continuous planning process years ago after growing frustrated with the pace of decision making. Continuous planning ensures that resources are being directed toward evolving priorities and away from initiatives that have grown less important. The dynamic nature of agile initiatives also requires that executives devise new ways of keeping everything aligned and maintaining enterprise-level visibility, for example, via widely accessible dashboards that connect metrics across the company and link individual team metrics to aggregated company-level metrics.

Create small, talent-rich teams working outside the hierarchy to address your most important priorities

These teams are given permission to use agile methods and processes and to work outside of the often energy-draining and slower-moving traditional processes and decision hierarchies. Many leading companies such as Airbnb, Spotify, Google, Amazon, and Microsoft have adopted agile as a way of managing innovation and product development. Self-managed teams with limited hierarchy and bureaucracy are explicit features of such organizational models.

AB InBev has an executive team that works in a more agile way, though the members probably did not study scrum before adopting this way of working; it is inherent to their leadership style and culture. The CEO and his leadership team share a joint table. Issues are worked on quickly and cross-functionally in a less formal, less bureaucratic environment. This means no one has to call a special meeting, and issues do not have to be worked through different functional silos and then reintegrated at the top. This type of management boosts the velocity of decision making.

Time-box your work and make extensive use of test-and-learn techniques

Working in smaller increments of focused time, typically one to four weeks, also accelerates decision velocity and the overall corporate metabolism. This works well when you have moved from a calendar-based to a continuous planning process. Using test-and-learn techniques with both customers and internal stakeholders allows companies to take minimum viable solutions and iterate on them quickly, abandoning weaker solutions for better ones. This rapid, hypothesis-focused, real-time testing creates early constructive feedback for the team and accelerates the development of solutions.

No company demonstrates this intense focus on speed better than Amazon, which puts these concepts into practice every day. Amazon makes extensive use of well-researched white papers to help focus the management team on critical decisions. At the outset of a meeting, individuals are given time to read the white papers in silence before thoroughly discussing the merits of a proposal. Not all decisions are treated equally. In his 2016 letter to the shareholders video, CEO Jeff Bezos said, "Many decisions are reversible, two-way doors. Those decisions can use a light-weight process. For those, so what if you're wrong?"

One key to making decision velocity and time-boxing possible is establishing the right burden of proof before action. We have seen many weaker companies where the greatest sin a manager could commit was not being able to answer every question the executive team asked, even if the answers to these questions would not have changed the decision. According to Bezos, "Most decisions should probably be made with somewhere around 70% of the information you wish you had. If you wait for 90%, in most cases, you're probably being slow. Plus, either way, you need to be good at quickly recognizing and correcting bad decisions. If you're good at course correcting, being wrong may be less costly than you think, whereas being slow is going to be expensive for sure."

While we have seen few leadership teams that have embraced all of these ideas equally in the C-suite, companies are increasingly adopting these practices. Making this change stick and permeate through successive layers in the organization requires a change in leadership styles, from command-and-control to models that rely on trust. For leaders, this means learning to let go and to rely on their teams to offer the right answers. Companies like Spotify, with its principle of "loosely coupled and tightly aligned," and Google, with its broad spans of control, have mastered these concepts. These behavioral changes will not happen without a concerted effort, but we believe that new leadership techniques are within reach of all open-minded and talented executives.

Take a moment to hold your leadership team and yourself up to a mirror. Agile, and the resulting decision velocity, starts at the top of the house. Senior leadership teams that lead in an agile manner and make high-velocity decisions will see these behaviors mimicked at lower levels in the organization. Failing to do this is the surest way to shorten the half-life of your company and make everyone, including yourself, miserable along the way. But if you develop leaders with the right mindset and an agile approach to management, you can get the maximum value out of your company's use of its scarcest resources—the time, talent, and energy of your workforce.

TAKEAWAYS

If your company is making the complicated transition from a traditional to an agile enterprise, your senior team should adopt the following practices:

✓ Think of all your corporate initiatives as a backlog, reprioritizing when new initiatives are added.

✓ Focus on fewer tasks and move from a calendar-based planning process to a continuous issue-based planning process.

✓ Supplement the traditional annual strategic planning cycle with real-time, issue-based planning to allocate resources more dynamically.

✓ Create small, talent-rich teams to address your highest priorities and boost the velocity of decision making.

✓ Work in small increments of focused time.

✓ Use test-and-learn techniques with both customers and internal stakeholders to accelerate the development of solutions.

Adapted from content posted on hbr.org, July 19, 2017 (product #H03SEK).

HOW AGILE TEAMS CAN HELP TURNAROUNDS SUCCEED

by Darrell K. Rigby, Simon Henderson, and Marco D'Avino

Agile—the management approach that relies on small, entrepreneurial, close-to-the-customer teams—has a reputation that reflects its rapid adoption in software development. It's for techies. It's for hip Silicon Valley startups. It is most definitely not for big, old-line companies that are facing an existential crisis and require a full-scale turnaround. In that situation, what you need is a clairvoyant dictator, someone who knows exactly what to do and can bring in the mercenaries to do it.

Let's look at these myths—for myths they are—in reverse order, dictator first.

Contrary to conventional wisdom and Hollywood action movies, dictatorial management is ineffective in large-scale crises. Command-and-control systems work best when operations are stable and predictable, commanders have greater knowledge of operating conditions and potential solutions than their subordinates do, centralized decision makers can effectively handle peak decision volumes, and sticking to standard operating procedures is more important than adapting to change.

None of these conditions exists in extreme events such as natural disasters, terrorist attacks, major military battles—or large-scale business turnarounds. The variability and unpredictability of events are too high for rigid directives. Experienced operators in the field have better knowledge and more current information than remote dictators or their mercenary agents do. Information overloads paralyze command centers, creating devastating bottlenecks. Standard operating procedures fail because the situations are by definition nonstandard.

Managers who fall prey to the dictator-in-a-crisis myth pay a heavy price. Their responses to unexpected developments are slow and ill-informed (think of Hurricane Katrina, the Chernobyl meltdown, perhaps even the demise of Sears). And their obvious lack of confidence in frontline employees will hinder growth long after the crisis passes.

For these reasons, modern crisis teams are turning from command-and-control systems to more adaptive, agile approaches. We have worked with some of these teams, and we have observed several others. All are putting that "hip" methodology to work in exactly the places where so many people have believed it was inappropriate.

An exemplar of the new approach is WorleyParsons, a global engineering and construction firm that specializes in oil field and other energy-related projects. In 2015, the price of oil dropped dramatically. Demand for WorleyParsons's services crashed, with oil and gas capital projects declining more than 50%. The company was suffering from lower revenue, declining margins, and a falling stock price. Large investments made when the market was growing, including several acquisitions, became a heavy debt load in the downturn.

As the crisis intensified, management undertook successive rounds of cost cuts. But the organization's energy and appetite for more cost-cutting was low. The company needed a new way of working, and when executives learned about agile, they decided to try it. Instead of issuing directives from the top, frontline management identified and set up initiatives that eventually involved hundreds of teams throughout the organization. These teams changed their ways of working. They structured their work in sprints with a regimented process to arrive at key decisions. They utilized backlog prioritization, daily huddles, and the other tools of the agile trade. Senior leaders helped clear away obstacles and tracked the teams' results.

The agile approach injected a level of speed and accountability not found in many business turnarounds. The teams attacked the cost base from multiple angles. They reduced unnecessary work and process inefficiencies, proposing and then implementing everything from an overhaul of the firm's IT infrastructure to a ban on business-class travel. Senior executives called on local teams to attack opportunities only they could see and address. Those teams accelerated responses to customers' requests for proposals, fixed ineffective and inefficient heating and cooling systems, consolidated duplicative support functions among regional and global operations, and fully owned the outcomes.

The results were both remarkable and quick. In the first 100 days, the firm increased its cash position by 20%, reduced its net debt, and registered a $120 million gain in anticipated profitability. After just one year, margins had increased by five percentage points, cost savings totaled $400 million (on an addressable cost base of $1.2 billion), and the stock price was up more than four-fold. Even more important, thousands of people had now participated in agile-based initiatives. They had learned new skills and gained new confidence. They were more and more focused on growing the top line and innovating, and launched new initiatives accordingly.

Employing agile in this kind of context does require adapting some conventional practices, and it adds some risk. For example, agile teams usually aim to provide their members with sustainable lifestyles and have them work at a pace that they can maintain indefinitely. In a turn-around, teams may work unsustainable hours for several months at a time. In ordinary circumstances, agile teams usually create a working increment every one to four weeks. In a turnaround, tough circumstances sometimes require creating working increments in a single day. In general, agile teams may be required to make decisions faster and with less information than traditional teams.

To mitigate such risks, agile turnaround leaders typically take five actions:

- **They communicate—even overcommunicate—the strategic ambition to a broader range of people.** Since leaders know they will be delegating far more decisions, they ensure that people making those decisions are fully aligned on what to do and why to do it. That way, how they do it can be flexible yet faithful to the strategy.

- **They serve as coaches, not commanders.** In a turn-around, people are afraid to make mistakes, so they bring decisions to their boss. Strong leaders act as coaches and trainers to expand the quantity and quality of decision makers.

- **They strengthen lines of communication among the teams.** To avoid becoming a bottleneck, they develop tools that help everyone see what all the teams are doing at any time.

- **They accelerate learning loops, emphasizing progress over perfection.** They embrace unpredictability and don't get slowed by excessive precision. Adequate approximations will do.

- **They shift measurement and reward systems to larger teams.** One of the biggest problems in a crisis is that people focus on doing what is best for the individuals they know and trust—which often means people in their own silos. Effective turnaround leaders enlarge circles of trust and collaboration.

In a conventional turnaround, a small team of people at the top tries to figure out a company's problems and make the necessary changes. In an agile turnaround, hundreds or even thousands of employees attack those problems at the root—and are learning skills they can put to work when the company recovers. The agile approach is indisputably better.

TAKEAWAYS

Turnarounds require making decisions faster with less information. Agile teams can help leaders reduce those risks by:

✓ Overcommunicating to a broader range of people to ensure that decision makers are aligned on what to do and why

✓ Acting as coaches and trainers to expand the quantity and quality of decision makers

✓ Strengthening the lines of communication so that everyone can see what all teams are doing at any time

✓ Accelerating learning, emphasizing progress over perfection

✓ Widening circles of trust and collaboration by shifting measurement and rewards systems to larger teams

Adapted from content posted on hbr.org, July 2, 2018 (product #H04F74).

8

MAKING PROCESS IMPROVEMENTS STICK

S tarting with Frederick Taylor and W. Edwards Deming, managers have long been obsessed with ways to improve business processes. And in the past 20 years, a host of improvement initiatives, including lean production, Six Sigma, and agile, have swept through a range of industries. Studies show that companies embracing such techniques may enjoy significant improvements in efficiency and costs. But when the University of North Carolina's Brad Staats and the University of Oxford's Matthias Holweg and David Upton looked at the benefits, they noticed a gap. "These things always work well initially, but often the gains fade very quickly," Holweg says. "It's always felt like researchers were telling only half the story. It's not just about putting the programs in place—it's also about making them stick."

To understand why some improvements are sustained and others aren't, the researchers examined 204 lean projects launched from 2012 to 2017 at a European bank with more than 2,000 branches in 14 countries and serving more than 16 million customers. The lean initiative, started by the head office, was supported by a global consulting firm, which helped create an in-house academy to train lean "champions" at each regional subsidiary. Initial projects focused on processes (such as opening an account and making a wire transfer) that could benefit from decreased handoffs and fewer steps and were common to all regions. The regional offices subsequently identified additional projects according to their needs. The projects shared an overarching goal: to increase labor productivity, a key variable in service operations.

At first glance, the initiative appeared to be a great success. Over the first four years, the bank launched 33 to 51 projects every six months, each involving 1,600 employees, on average. Initial improvements in efficiency averaged 10%; the gains rose to 20% after a year and 31% after two years. Those numbers are in line with the best-performing lean implementations in any industry, the researchers say, and the bank was rightly very pleased.

But when the researchers looked more closely, they found a more complicated picture. Despite the impressive aggregate gains, 21% of projects failed to yield any improvements. And among the 79% that showed initial improvements, many regressed: Only 73% were still producing results above baseline after a year, and after two years the number fell to 44%. Adding up the projects that had no improvements and the ones for which improvements were temporary, only slightly more than one-third of projects held on to gains after two years.

The researchers also explored whether projects that were initially successful could not only preserve the gains but also show continuous improvement—getting progressively better over time, which is the goal of many lean projects. Just 51% of them were continuing to improve a year after launch; after two years the figure dropped to 36%.

Seeking to understand these findings, the researchers looked at factors identified in previous research as influencing the initial success of lean projects: the experience of local leaders driving implementation, the level of training provided, and teams' familiarity in working together. None explained the difference, suggesting that what accounts for initial success is different from what's needed to hold on to gains or to improve further.

Interviews with lean champions in the bank's 14 countries provided some insight. Managers said that one condition needed to keep improving was visible support from board members and senior leadership—without it, frontline workers believe that the company's enthusiasm for the effort has waned, and backsliding ensues. They also cited the need for consistent measurement and monitoring and noted that problems arise when significant early improvements give way to diminishing returns. "Addressing the low-hanging fruit is easy; it becomes harder in the long term," one lean champion told the researchers.

The data reinforces these observations. Projects with strong support from the head office showed 35% greater improvement after a year than ones without that support; they were also less likely to backslide, with 79% performing above baseline after a year, compared with 61% of projects not driven by the head office. "Senior leadership, through paying attention to the lean improvements, clearly has a major enabling role in sustaining improvements," the researchers write. Some companies hope that a continuous-improvement mentality will become embedded in their culture and will motivate frontline workers even without the involvement of senior leaders, but this work suggests that hope may be unrealistic. (See the sidebar "'Leaders Must Make Sense of These Things': In Practice with Helen Bevans.")

"Leaders Must Make Sense of These Things": In Practice with Helen Bevan

Helen Bevan has spent 25 years overseeing change initiatives at England's National Health Service, which serves more than 50 million patients and employs 1.2 million health care staffers. She spoke with HBR about the challenges of preserving the gains from one initiative while launching new efforts. Edited excerpts follow.

Why is it so hard to sustain an initiative's improvements?

It's an issue of energy. And when a new initiative comes along, people ask, "What do we do with the old one?" Much of our workforce models the behavior of senior leaders, and when those leaders shift their energy to something else, it's hard to sustain things.

What differentiates changes that stick?

Sustainability starts at the beginning, in how we frame a project and what it means to the organization and our purpose. It's the difference between behaving like a buyer and behaving like an investor. If we're asking doctors to get on board something that's underway,

(continued)

it's already too late. We need to get them invested in the project, and thinking like owners, well before it begins. When I look at the difference between projects that are sustained and ones that aren't, it often has to do with taking the time at the beginning to set them up, frame them the right way, and get people invested.

Is this especially hard in a health care setting, where efficiencies may seem to conflict with quality care?
Our purpose is health and wellness. That's what motivates people in this sector; they don't come for the pay. If we can frame a project as relating to things that really matter to the people who work here, they will connect with it on an emotional level. Even doctors, who make decisions logically, are more likely to engage and be motivated if an initiative fits with their emotions and values. So we show data and avoid jargon. If we talk about "lean" and "agile" and use words like *kanban*, *kaizen*, and *scrum*, it feels like we're taking away people's autonomy. We can convey those concepts perfectly well without those words.

But don't people worry that the programs are actually about cost cutting?

Of course we focus on costs—we have finite resources. But it's about framing. Instead of talking about waste, we focus on unwarranted variation in care. Every patient with the same condition should get the same high-quality treatment; when that doesn't happen, it can be a matter of life and death. Variation also adds to cost, so reducing unwarranted variation increases care and reduces cost. We see more success when we frame things in terms of our mission, which is care.

How do you start an initiative without losing the gains of the previous one?

Four years ago we did a crowdsourcing exercise in which we asked colleagues about the biggest barriers to change. The most common answer was "confusing strategies." People said that when a new initiative, target, goal, or focus comes along, they don't know whether it's more important than the previous one. We have to find ways to continue the journeys we've started by sustaining people's energy while creating space for new things. Managers and leaders must make sense of those things and reduce ambiguity.

The researchers also interviewed executives with deep experience leading lean initiatives across a range of industries; from this, they identified three ways in which organizations can help initiatives achieve sustained improvements.

The first is by communicating the program in a clear narrative that aligns with the organization's purpose. For example, a hotel might focus on how a lean process will improve guest satisfaction; that's more likely to motivate employees than an emphasis on cost savings. The second is by directing efforts toward pain points whose easing would clearly benefit employees. For instance, one hospital's initiative aimed to decrease the time medical personnel spent on paperwork, freeing them up for patient care. The third is by ensuring that senior leaders act as coaches, enabling small wins to increase employees' motivation and engagement.

A particularly troublesome obstacle to sustained improvement, the researchers say, is initiative fatigue, which occurs when leaders jump too quickly from one improvement fad to another. (One of the researchers has joked about the danger of airport bookstores, which tempt traveling executives to pick up business books that may send them in pursuit of a new improvement plan.) Embarking on a new project is often more exciting than staying the course, but that doesn't necessarily deliver the best long-term results. Staats says, "It's always easier to start something, whether it's weight loss, going to the gym, or smoking cessation. Getting individual changes to stick is hard, and getting organizational changes to stick is even harder."

TAKEAWAYS

Putting a process improvement such as agile in place isn't the only challenge—you also need to make it stick. According to research by University of North Carolina's Brad Staats and the University of Oxford's Matthias Holweg and David Upton, there are three key things you can do to make organizational changes last. To help initiatives achieve sustained improvements:

- ✓ Communicate the program with clear messaging that aligns with the organization's purpose

- ✓ Direct efforts toward addressing pain points that most directly impact employees

✓ Ensure senior leaders act as coaches to achieve small wins and increase employees' motivation and engagement

Reprinted from Harvard Business Review, *November–December 2018 (product #F1806A).*

About the Contributors

PETER CAPPELLI is the George W. Taylor Professor of Management at the Wharton School and a director of its Center for Human Resources.

ALIA CROCKER is an assistant professor of strategy at Babson College. She researches and consults on issues related to strategic human capital.

ROB CROSS is the Edward A. Madden Professor of Global Leadership at Babson College. He is a coauthor of *The Hidden Power of Social Networks* (Harvard Business Review Press, 2004) and author of a forthcoming book on improving the effectiveness of collaboration (Harvard Business Review Press).

MARCO D'AVINO is a Bain partner based in Sydney and a leader in Bain Accelerated Transformation.

NEEL DOSHI is a coauthor of the *New York Times* best-selling book *Primed to Perform: How to Build the Highest*

Performing Cultures through the Science of Total Motivation, and cofounder of Vega Factor, a startup that helps organizations transform their cultures. Previously, Neel was a partner at McKinsey & Company. He received his MBA from Wharton and BS from MIT.

HEIDI K. GARDNER is a distinguished fellow at the Center on the Legal Profession and faculty chair of the Accelerated Leadership Program at Harvard Law School. She is the author of *Smart Collaboration: How Professionals and Their Firms Succeed by Breaking Down Silos* (Harvard Business Review Press, 2017).

ERIC GARTON is a partner in Bain & Company's Chicago office and leader of the firm's Global Organization practice. He is a coauthor of *Time, Talent, Energy: Overcome Organizational Drag and Unleash Your Team's Productive Power* (Harvard Business Review Press, 2017).

SIMON HENDERSON is a Bain partner based in Sydney and the global leader of Bain Accelerated Transformation.

LINDSAY MCGREGOR is a coauthor of the *New York Times* best-selling book, *Primed to Perform: How to Build the Highest Performing Cultures through the Science of Total Motivation,* as well as the CEO and cofounder of Vega

Factor, a startup that helps organizations transform their cultures. Previously, Lindsay led projects at McKinsey & Company. She received her MBA from Harvard Business School and her BA from Princeton.

ANDY NOBLE is a partner in Bain & Company's organization practice and is located in the Boston office.

DARRELL K. RIGBY is a partner in the Boston office of Bain & Company. He heads the firm's global innovation practice. He is the author of *Winning in Turbulence* (Harvard Business Review Press, 2009) and a coauthor of the forthcoming *Doing Agile Right: Transformation Without Chaos* (Harvard Business Review Press, 2020).

PHIL SIMON is a frequent keynote speaker, Slack trainer, and recognized technology authority. He is the award-winning author of nine management books, most recently *Slack for Dummies*. He also teaches full-time at Arizona State University. Find out more about him at www.philsimon.com.

JEFF SUTHERLAND is a cocreator of the scrum form of agile innovation and the CEO of Scrum Inc., a consulting and training firm.

ANNA TAVIS is a clinical associate professor of human capital management at New York University and the Perspectives editor at *People + Strategy*, a journal for HR executives.

Index

agility
  building across the business,
    17–25
  points of execution, 45–46
Amazon, xii, 2, 13, 18, 19, 83,
    97, 99
analytics, 52. *See also*
  collaboration
annual appraisals, 23, 69, 71–72
annual planning, 24–25, 96
ANZ, 93
Apple, 96
apps, for feedback, 80–81.
  See also feedback
artificial intelligence and HR,
  86. *See also* human
  resources (HR)
Ascendify, 85

backlog, enterprise priorities
  as, 95–97
Bain & Company, 94
Bank of Montreal (BMO), 68,
  70, 81
Bevan, Helen, 115–117
Bezos, Jeff, 13, 99
Bosch, xiii, 5–7, 18
boundary spanners, 46, 53–55.
  See also agile teams
budgeting cycles, 24–25
bureaucracy, xi, 2, 3, 4, 8, 18,
  24, 68–69, 97

businesses
  operating architectures of,
    19–23
  planning and budgeting
    cycles of, 24–25
  talent acquisition and
    motivation in, 23–24
  values and principles of,
    18–19, 26

Cappelli, Peter, 67–92
Cardinal Health, 96
change
  adapting to, 4
  barriers to, 117
  big-bang, 12–13
  management of, 73–74
  sustaining initiatives, 111–120
C. H. Robinson, xii–xiii
Cigna, 75–76
Cisco, 80, 82, 85
coaching, 23, 75–77, 90, 91, 108
collaboration, 37–39, 43–57
command-and-control
  management, 100, 104–105
communication, 107–108. *See
  also* information, exchange of
compensation systems, 24, 69,
  82–84, 91
Connected Commons, 44
constraints, 10, 12. *See also*
  agile methods, scaling up

Is Your Business Ready for the Future?

If you enjoyed this book and want more on today's pressing business topics, turn to other books in the **Insights You Need** series from *Harvard Business Review*. Featuring HBR's latest thinking on topics critical to your company's success—from Blockchain and Cybersecurity to AI and Agile—each book will help you explore these trends and how they will impact you and your business in the future.

FOR MORE VISIT HBR.ORG/BOOKS

The most important management ideas all in one place.

We hope you enjoyed this book from *Harvard Business Review*. Now you can get even more with HBR's 10 Must Reads Boxed Set. From books on leadership and strategy to managing yourself and others, this 6-book collection delivers articles on the most essential business topics to help you succeed.

HBR's 10 Must Reads Series

The definitive collection of ideas and best practices on our most sought-after topics from the best minds in business.

- Change Management
- Collaboration
- Communication
- Emotional Intelligence
- Innovation
- Leadership
- Making Smart Decisions

- Managing Across Cultures
- Managing People
- Managing Yourself
- Strategic Marketing
- Strategy
- Teams
- The Essentials

hbr.org/mustreads

Buy for your team, clients, or event.
Visit hbr.org/bulksales for quantity discount rates.

Harvard
Business
Review
Press